THE GREEK TRAVELMATE

compiled by
LEXUS
with
Irene M Cavoura

RICHARD DREW PUBLISHING
Glasgow

RICHARD DREW PUBLISHING LTD.
6 CLAIRMONT GARDENS
GLASGOW G3 7LW
SCOTLAND

First Published 1982
First Reprint April 1982
Second Reprint May 1984
Third Reprint May 1985
New Edition 1986

ISBN 0 904002 78 0

Printed and bound in Great Britain by
Cox & Wyman Ltd.

YOUR TRAVELMATE

gives you one single easy-to-use list of useful words and phrases to help you communicate in Greek.

Built into this list are:

– Travel Tips with facts and figures which provide valuable information

– typical replies to some of the things you might want to say.

And on page 125 you'll find a list of Greek words that you'll see on signs and notices.

There is a menu reader on pages 69–71. Numbers are on pages 126–127 and the Greek alphabet is on page 128.

Your TRAVELMATE also tells you how to pronounce Greek. Just read the pronunciations as though they were English and you will communicate – although you might not sound like a native speaker.

Some notes on Greek sounds:

th is like 'th' in 'theatre' as against 'th' in 'there'

kh is pronounced like the 'ch' in Scottish 'loch'

e should be pronounced as in 'wet'

o should be pronounced as in 'hot'

Vowels in italics show which part of a word to stress.

You'll notice that a semi-colon is the Greek question mark.

Your TRAVELMATE gives the pronunciation before the actual Greek characters. And this way of writing Greek with English characters can in fact be used for telegrams etc.

a, an *enas, meea, ena* [ἕνας, μία, ἕνα]

    20 drachmas a kilo *eekosee thraxmes to keelo*
[εἴκοσι δραχμές τό κιλό]

abdomen *ee keeleea* [ἡ κοιλιά]

aboard: aboard the ship/plane *pano sto
pleeo/aereplano* [πάνω στό πλοίο/ἀεροπλάνο]

about: is he about? *eene etho?* [εἶναι ἐδῶ;]

    about 15 *pereepoo theka pende* [περίπου 15]

    about 2 o'clock *pereepoo theeoee ora* [περίπου
2 ἡ ὥρα]

above *apo pano* [ἀπό πάνω]

abroad *sto exotereeko* [στό ἐξωτερικό]

absolutely! *opostheepote* [ὁπωσδήποτε]

accelerator *to gazee* [τό γκάζι]

accept *thekhome* [δέχομαι]

accident *ena theesteekheema* [ἕνα δυστύχημα]

    there's been an accident *eyeene ena
theesteekheema* [ἔγινε ἕνα δυστύχημα]

accommodation *thomateeo* [δωμάτιο]

    we need accommodation for three *thelome
thomateea yeea trees* [θέλομε δωμάτια γιά τρεῖς]

accurate *akreevees* [ἀκριβής]

ache: my back aches *ponaee ee platee moo*
[πονάει ἡ πλάτη μου]

across *apenandee* [ἀπέναντι]

    how do we get across? *pos tha pame
apenandee?* [πῶς θά πᾶμε ἀπέναντι;]

adaptor *ena polaplo* [ἕνα πολλαπλό]

address *ee thee-ef-theensee* [ἡ διεύθυνση]

    will you give me your address? *tha moo
thosete teen thee-ef-theensee sas* [θά μοῦ δώσετε
τήν διεύθυνσή σας;]

adjust *reethmeezo* [ρυθμίζω]

admission *ee eesothos* [ἡ εἴσοδος]

advance: can we book in advance? boroome na kleesoome *the*sees apo preen? [μπορούμε νά κλείσουμε θέσεις ἀπό πρίν;]

advert m*ee*a theea*fee*meessee [μία διαφήμιση]

afraid: I'm afraid I don't know then χero [δέν ξέρω]

    I'm afraid so ne [ναί]

    I'm afraid not okhee [ὄχι]

after: after you meta apo sas [μετά ἀπό σᾶς]

    after 2 o'clock meta tees th*eeo ee*ora [μετά τίς δύο ἡ ὥρα]

afternoon to apo-yevma [τό ἀπόγευμα]

    in the afternoon to apo-yevma [τό ἀπόγευμα]

    good afternoon kaleespera [καλησπέρα]

    this afternoon af*to* to apo-yevma [αὐτό τό ἀπόγευμα]

aftershave koloneea xeer*ee*smatos [κολώνια ξυρίσματος]

again xan*a* [ξανά]

against enand*ee*on [ἐναντίον]

age ee eeleek*ee*a [ἡ ἡλικία]

    under age an*ee*leekos [ἀνήλικος]

    it takes ages ka*n*nee pol*ee* ora [κάνει πολύ ὥρα]

ago: a week ago teen peresm*e*nee evthomatha [τήν περασμένη ἐβδομάδα]

    it wasn't long ago then pa*ee* pol*ee*s keros [δέν πάει πολύς καιρός]

    how long ago was that? preen poso kero *ee*tan af*to* [πρίν πόσο καιρό ἦταν αὐτό]

agree: I agree seemfon*o* [συμφωνῶ]

    garlic doesn't agree with me to skortho then me ofel*ee* [τό σκόρδο δέν μέ ὠφελεῖ]

air o a-eras [ὁ ἀέρας]

    by air aeroporeekos [ἀεροπορικῶς]

    with air-conditioning me kleemateesm*o* [μέ κλιματισμό]

airport to aerothrom*ee*o [τό ἀεροδρόμειο]

alarm o seenagermos [ὁ συναγερμός]

    alarm clock to xeepneet*ee*ree [τό ξυπνητήρι]

alcohol to alkool [τό ἀλκοόλ]
  is it alcoholic? *ee*ne alkool*ee*ko? [εἶναι
  ἀλκοολικό;]
alive: is he still alive? *ee*ne akoma zondanos?
  [εἶναι ἀκόμα ζωντανός;]
all ola [ὅλα]
  all these people olee aft*ee* ee *anth*ropee [ὅλοι
  αὐτοί οἱ ἄνθρωποι]
  that's all aft*a* *ee*ne ola [αὐτά εἶναι ὅλα]
  that's all wrong *ee*ne *lath*os [εἶναι λάθος]
  all right ent*a*xee [ἐντάξη]
  thank you – not at all ef-khar*ee*sto – parakal*o*
  [εὐχαριστῶ – παρακαλῶ]
allergic: I'm allergic to penicillin *ee*me
  aleryek*o*s stee peneekeel*ee*nee [εἶμαι
  ἀλεργικός στή πενικιλλίνη]
allowed: is it allowed? epeetr*e*pete?
  [ἐπιτρέπεται;]
  that's not allowed aft*o* then epeetr*e*pete
  [αὐτό δέν ἐπιτρέπεται]
  allow me epeetr*e*pste moo [ἐπιτρέψτε μου]
almost sk*eth*on [σχεδόν]
alone monos [μόνος]
  did you come here alone? *eerth*ate etho
  monos sas? [εἴρθατε ἐδώ μόνος σας;]
  leave me alone *a*se me *ee*seekhee [ἄσε με
  ἤσυχη]
already *ee*thee [ἤδη]
also ep*ee*sees [ἐπίσης]
alternator metaskheematees*stee*s
  [μετασχιματιστής]
although anke [ἄνκαι]
**altogether: what does that make
  altogether?** poso kanoon ola maz*ee*? [πόσο
  κάνουν ὅλα μαζί;]
always panda [πάντα]
a.m. pro meseemvr*ee*eas [πρό μεσημβρίας π.μ.]
ambassador o presvees [ό πρέσβυς]
ambulance to proton voee*th*eeon [τό πρώτων
  βοηθειῶν]

....

get an ambulance! kaleste to proton
voee*thee*on! [καλέστε τό πρώτων βοηθειῶν!]
» *TRAVEL TIP: to get an ambulance dial 100 for the
police*
America Amereek*ee* [Ἀμερική]
American Amereekan*os* [Ἀμερικανός]
among metax*ee* [μεταξύ]
amp: 15 amp fuse mee*a* asf*a*leea theka p*e*nde
amp*er* [μιά ἀσφάλεια δέκα πέντε ἀμπέρ]
anchor ee *a*ngeera [ἡ ἄγκυρα]
and ke [καί]
angry *th*eemom*e*nos [θυμωμένος]
   I'm very angry about it *ee*me pol*ee*
   *th*eemom*e*nos yee-aft*o* [εἶμαι πολύ θυμωμένος
   γι' αὐτό]
   please don't get angry sas parakal*o* mee
   *th*eem*o*nete [σᾶς παρακαλῶ μή θυμώνετε]
animal to zo-o [τό ζῶο]
ankle o astr*a*galos [ὁ ἀστράγαλος]
anniversary: it's our anniversary eene ee
   epetee*o*s mas [εἶναι ἡ ἐπέτειός μας]
annoy: he's annoying me me enokhl*ee* [μέ
   ἐνοχλεῖ]
   it's very annoying *ee*ne pol*ee* enokhleeteeko
   [εἶναι πολύ ἐνοχλητικό]
another: can we have another room?
   bor*oo*me na *e*khome *e*na *a*lo thom*a*teeo?
   [μποροῦμε νά ἔχωμε ἕνα ἄλλο δωμάτειο;]
   another beer, please *a*lee mee*a* beera
   p*a*rakal*o* [ἄλλη μία μπύρα παρακαλῶ]
answer: what was his answer? tee
   ap*a*ndeese? [τί ἀπάντησε;]
   there was no answer then eep*e*erkhe
   ap*a*ndeesee [δέν ὑπῆρχε ἀπάντηση]
any: have you got any bananas/butter?
   *e*khete ban*a*nes/v*oo*teero? [ἔχετε
   μπανάνες/βούτυρο;]
   I haven't got any then*e*kho k*a*thol*o* [δέν ἔχω
   καθόλου]
anybody kan*ee*s [κανείς]

can anybody help? bor*ee* kan*ee*s na
voee*thee*see? [μπορεῖ κανεὶς νά βοηθήσει;]
anything otee*thee*pote [ὀτιδήποτε]
I don't want anything then *the*lo teepote [δέν
θέλω τίποτε]
aperitif *e*na aperit*if* [ἕνα ἀπεριτίφ]
apology: please accept my apologies zeet*o*
seegnomee [ζητῶ συγγνώμη]
I want an apology *the*lo na moo zeet*ee*sete
seegnomee [θέλω νά μοῦ ζητήσετε συγγνώμη]
appendicitis sko-leeko-eet*hee*tees
[σκωληκοειδῖτις]
appetite *o*rex*ee* [ὄρεξη]
I've lost my appetite *e*khasa teen *o*rex*ee* moo
[ἔχασα τήν ὄρεξή μου]
apple *e*na m*ee*lo [ἕνα μῆλο]
application form m*ee*a etee*see* [μία αἴτηση]
appointment: can I make an appointment?
bor*o* na kl*ee*sso *e*na ranver*oo*? [μπορῶ νά
κλείσω ἕνα ραντεβοὖ;]
apricot *e*na ver*ee*koko [ἕνα βερύκοκκο]
April Apr*ee*leeos ['Απρίλιος]
aqualung book*a*les oxigon*oo* [μπουκάλες
ὀξυγόνου]
archaeology arkheo-loy*ee*a [ἀρχαιολογία]
area ee pereeokh*ee* [ἡ περιοχή]
in the area steen pereeokh*ee* [στήν περιοχή]
arm to kher*ee* [τό χέρι]
around *see* **about**
arrange: will you arrange it? *tha* to
kanon*ee*sete? [θά τό κανονίσετε;]
it's all arranged ola *ee*ne kanoneezm*e*na [ὅλα
εἶναι κανονισμένα]
arrest (verb) seelamv*a*no [συλλαμβάνω]
he's been arrested ton seel*a*vane [τόν
συλλάβανε]
arrival ee *a*feexee [ἡ ἄφιξη]
arrive f*tha*no [φθάνω]
we only arrived yesterday f*tha*-same mo lees
kh*the*s [φθάσαμε μόλις χθές]

....

art tekhnee [τέχνη]

art gallery moosseeo [μουσείο]

arthritis ar-three-teeka [ἀρθριτικά]

artificial tekhneeto [τεχνητό]

artist o kaleetekhnees [ὁ καλλιτέχνης]

as: as quickly as you can oso pio greegora
borees [ὅσο πιό γρήγορα μπορεῖς]

  as much as you can oso pio polee borees [ὅσο
  πιό πολύ μπορεῖς]

  do as I do kane otee kano ego [κάνε ὅτι κάνω
  ἐγώ]

  as you like opos thelees [ὅπως θέλεις]

ashore steeh kseera [στήν ξηρά]

ashtray ena tasakee [ἔνα τασάκι]

ask roto [ρωτῶ]

  could you ask him to . . .? borees na too
  zeeteessees na . . .? [μπορεῖς νά τοῦ ζητήσεις
  νά . . .]

  that's not what I asked for theneene afto poo
  zeeteessa [δέν εἶναι αὐτό πού ζήτησα]

asleep: he's still asleep akomee keemate
[ἀκόμη κοιμᾶται]

asparagus sparanghee [σπαράγγι]

aspirin meea aspeereenee [μιά ἀσπιρίνη]

assistant o voeethos [ὁ βοηθός]

asthma asthma [ἄσθμα]

at: at the cafe sto zakharoplasteeo [στό
ζαχαροπλαστεῖο]

  at my hotel sto xenothokheeo moo [στό
  ξενοδοχεῖο μου]

  at one o'clock stees meea ee ora [στίς μία ἡ
  ὥρα]

Athens Atheena [᾽Αθήνα]

atmosphere ee atmosfera [ἡ ἀτμόσφαιρα]

attitude enas tropos [ἔνας τρόπος]

attractive oreo [ὡραῖο]

  (person) elkeesteeko [ἑλκυστικό]

  I think you're very attractive nomeezo otee
  eese polee elkeesteekee [νομίζω ὅτι εἶσαι πολύ
  ἑλκυστική]

aubergine mee*a* meleedza*n*a [μιά μελιτζάνα]
August *A*vgoostos [Αὔγουστος]
aunt ee *th*ee*a* [ἡ θεία μου]
Australia Afstralee*a* [Αὐστραλία]
Australian Afstralos [Αὐστραλός]
authorities ee arkh*e*s [οἱ ἀρχές]
automatic *(car)* *e*na aft*o*mato [ἕνα αὐτόματο]
autumn: in the autumn to *fth*eenoporo [τό
    φθινόπωρο]
away: is it far away from here? ee*n*e makree*a*
    apo tho? [εἶναι μακριά ἀπό δῶ;]
    go away! *fee*-ye! [φύγε!]
awful tromer*o* [τρομερό]
axle o *a*xonas [ὁ ἄξωνας]
baby to mor*o* [τό μωρό]
    we'd like a baby-sitter *the*lome mee*a*
    baby-sitter [θέλομε μιά baby-σίτερ]
» *TRAVEL TIP: baby-sitters can be hired by the hour*
    through travel agencies and hotels
back: I've got a bad back pon*a*ee ee pl*a*tee
    moo [πονάει ἡ πλάτη μου]
    I'll be back soon *th*a yee-ree*so* greegora [θά
    γυρίσω γρήγορα]
    is he back? ekhee ye-ree*ss*ee? [ἔχει γυρίσει;]
    come back yee-rna pee*ss*o [γύρνα πίσω]
    can I have my money back? bor*o* na *e*kho ta
    lef*ta* moo pee*ss*o? [μπορῶ νά ἔχω τά λεφτά μου
    πίσω;]
    I go back tomorrow *th*a pa*o* pee*ss*o*a*vree*o* [θά
    πάω πίσω αὔριο]
    at the back sto pee*ss*o m*e*ros [στό πίσω μέρος]
bacon bakon [μπέϊκον]
    bacon and eggs avg*a* me bakon [αὐγά μέ
    μπέϊκον]
bad *a*s-kheema [ἄσχημα]
    it's not bad th*e*n ee*n*e as-kheema [δέν εἶναι
    ἄσχημα]
    too bad pol*ee* *a*s-kheema [πολύ ἄσχημα]
bag ee ts*a*nda [ἡ τσάντα]
    (suitcase) ee val*ee*dsa [ἡ βαλίτσα]

baggage ee aposkev*es* [οἱ ἀποσκευές]

baker's o foorn*a*rees [ὁ φουρνάρης]

balcony to balk*o*nee [τό μπαλκόνι]

a room with a balcony ena thom*a*teeo me balk*o*nee [ἕνα δωμάτιο μέ μπαλκόνι]

ball ee b*a*la [ἡ μπάλλα]

ball-point pen ena beek [ἕνα μπίκ]

banana m*ee*a ban*a*na [μιά μπανάνα]

band orkh*ee*stra [ὀρχήστρα]

bandage o ep*ee*thesmos [ὁ ἐπίδεσμος]

could you change the bandage? bor*ee*te na al*a*xete ton ep*ee*thesmo? [μπορεῖτε νά ἀλλάξετε τόν ἐπίδεσμο;]

bank ee tr*a*peza [ἡ τράπεζα]

» *TRAVEL TIP: banking hours: Mon—Fri 8.00-14.00 hrs; you'll need your passport at the bank; bank holidays see public holidays; money can also be changed at points of entry into Greece (24 hr service), at some Telecommunication Offices (OTE) and post offices and at some hotels and in tourist gift shops*

YOU MAY HEAR...

to the*ea*vate*e*reeo sas parakal*o* *your passport please*

bar to b*a*r [μπάρ]

when does the bar open? pote an*ee*gee to b*a*r? [πότε ἀνοίγει τό μπάρ;]

barber's o korr*ea*s [ὁ κουρέας]

bargain: it's a real bargain pragmatee*kee* efker*ee*a [εἶναι πραγματική εὐκαιρία]

barmaid ee serv*ee*tora [ἡ σερβιτόρα]

barman o b*a*rman [ὁ μπάρμαν]

basket to kal*a*thee [τό καλάθι]

bath to b*a*neeo [τό μπάνιο]

can I have a bath? boro na k*a*no b*a*neeo? [μπορῶ νά κάνω μπάνιο;]

could you give me a bath towel? moo the*e*nete m*ee*a petss*e*ta b*a*neeoo? [μου δίνετε μία πετσέτα μπάνιου;]

bathing to koleembee [τό κολύμβι]
   bathing costume to ma-yo [τό μαγιό]
bathroom to lootro [τό λουτρό]
   we want a room with a private bathroom
   *the*lome ena thoma*tee*o me lootro [θέλομε ἕνα
   δωμάτιο μέ λουτρό]
   can I use your bathroom? boro na
   khree-ss*ee*-mo-pee-*ee*sso to lootro sas? [μπορῶ
   νά χρησιμοποιήσω τό λουτρό σας;]
battery ee batar*ee*a [ἡ μπαταρία]
beach ee paral*ee*a [ἡ παραλία]
   see you on the beach *tha* se tho steen
   paral*ee*a [θά σέ δῶ στήν παραλία]
beans fass*o*leea [φασόλια]
beautiful oreos [ὡραῖος]
   that was a beautiful meal *ee*tan ena oreo
   ye-vma [ἦταν ἕνα ὡραῖο γεῦμα]
because epeeth*ee* [ἐπειδή]
   because of the weather logo too keroo [λόγω
   τοῦ καιροῦ]
bed kreva*tee* [τό κρεβάτι]
   single bed/double bed mono kreva*tee*/
   theeplo kreva*tee* [μονό κρεβάτι/διπλό κρεβάτι]
   you haven't changed my bed then*a*laxate to
   kreva*tee* moo [δέν ἀλλάξατε τό κρεβάτι μου]
   bed and breakfast thoma*tee*o me pro-eeno
   [δωμάτιο μέ πρωϊνό]
   I want to go to bed *the*lo na ksaplosso [θέλω
   νά ξαπλώσω]
bedroom to eepnothoma*tee*o [τό ὑπνοδωμάτιο]
bee meea meleessa [μιά μέλισσα]
beef moskha*ree* [μοσχάρι]
beer meea beera [μιά μπύρα]
   two beers, please theeo bee*res*, parakalo [δυό
   μπύρες, παρακαλῶ]
before: before breakfast preen to proeeno
   [πρίν τό πρωϊνό]
   before we leave preen feegome [πρίν φύγομε]
   I haven't been here before then ekho
   ksan*ar*th*ee* etho [δέν ἔχω ξανάρθει ἐδῶ]

....

begin: when does it begin? pote arkh*ee*zee?
[πότε ἀρχίζει;]

beginner arkh*a*reeos [ἀρχάριος]

behind p*ee*sso [πίσω]

  the car behind me to aftok*ee*neeto p*ee*sso moo
  [τό αὐτοκίνητο πίσω μου]

believe: I don't believe you then se peest*evo*
[δέν σέ πιστεύω]

  I believe you se peest*evo* [σέ πιστεύω]

bell *(in hotel)* to kooth*oo*nee [τό κουδούνι]

belong: that belongs to me ek*ee*no*ee*ene theek*o*
moo [ἐκεῖνο εἶναι δικό μου]

  who does this belong to? pee-a-n*oo* eene aft*o*?
  [ποιανοῦ εἶναι αὐτό;]

below k*a*to [κάτω]

belt ee z*o*nee [ἡ ζώνη]

bend *(noun: in road)* ee strof*ee* [ἡ στροφή]

berries m*oo*ra [μούρα]

berth *(on ship)* mee*a* kl*ee*nee [μιά κλίνη]

beside thee*p*la [δίπλα]

best pol*ee* kal*ee*teros [πολύ καλλίτερος]

  it's the best holiday I've ever had *ee*ne ee
  kal*ee*teres theeakopes poo *ee*kha pot*e* [εἶναι οἱ
  καλλίτερες διακοπές ποῦ εἶχα ποτέ]

better kal*ee*tera [καλλίτερα]

  haven't you got anything better? then
  *e*khete t*ee*pote kal*ee*tero? [δέν ἔχετε τίποτε
  καλλίτερο;]

  are you feeling better? es-*th*aneste
  kal*ee*tera? [αἰσθάνεστε καλλίτερα;]

  I'm feeling a lot better es-*th*anome pol*ee*
  kal*ee*tera [αἰσθάνομαι πολύ καλλίτερα]

between metax*ee* [μεταξύ]

beyond p*e*ra [πέρα]

bicycle *e*na poth*ee*lato [ἕνα ποδήλατο]

  can we hire bicycles here? bor*oo*me na
  neek*ee*-a*s*ome poth*ee*lata etho? [μπορούμε νά
  νοικιάσωμε ποδήλατα ἐδῶ;]

big meg*a*lo [μεγάλο]

  a big one *e*na meg*a*lo [ἕνα μεγάλο]

that's too big eene polee megalo [είναι πολύ μεγάλο]

it's not big enough then eene arketa megalo [δέν είναι άρκετά μεγάλο]

have you got a bigger one? ekhete ena megaleetero? [έχετε ἕνα μεγαλλίτερο;]

bikini to bikini [τό μπικίνι]

bill o logareeasmos [ὁ λογαριασμός]

could I have the bill, please? boro na ekho ton logareeasmo, parakalo? [μπορῶ νά ἔχω τόν λογαριασμό, παρακαλῶ;]

bird to poolee [τό πουλί]

birthday ta ye-nethleea [τά γενέθλια]

happy birthday khroneea polla [χρόνια πολλά]

it's my birthday eene ta yenethleea moo [είναι τά γενέθλια μου]

biscuit beeskoto [μπισκότο]

bit: just a little bit for me mono leego ya mena [μόνο λίγο γιά μένα]

that's a bit too expensive afto eene kapos polee akreevo [αὐτό είναι κάπως πολύ άκριβό]

a bit of that cake leego apo afto to cake [λίγο ἀπό αὐτό τό κέϊκ]

a big bit ena megalo komatee [ἕνα μεγάλο κομμάτι]

bite: I've been bitten me thaghasse [μέ δάγκασε]

(by insect) me tsseembeesse [μέ στίμπησε]

bitter *(taste)* peekro [πικρό]

black mavro [μαῦρο]

he's had a blackout leepotheemeesse [λιποθύμησε]

bland ee-pee-os [ἤπιος]

blanket ee kooverta [ἡ κουβέρτα]

I'd like another blanket tha eethela alee meea kooberta [θά εἴθελα ἄλλη μία κουβέρτα]

bleach ee khlo-reenee [ἡ χλωρίνη]

bleed emorago [αἱμοραγῶ]

he's bleeding emoragee [αἱμοραγεῖ]

bless you *(after sneeze)* ya soo [γειά σου]

blind teeflos [τυφλός]

blind spot seemeeo khorees oratoteeta [σημεῖο χωρίς ὁρατότητα]

blister ee fooskala [ἡ φουσκάλα]

blocked fragmenos [φραγμένος]

blonde *(noun)* ksan*th*ee [ξανθή]

blood to ema [τό αἷμα]

his blood group is . . . ee om*a*tha too ematos too*ee*ne . . . [ἡ ὁμάδα τοῦ αἵματός του εἶναι . . .]

I've got high blood pressure ekho pseel*ee* pee-essee [ἔχω ψηλή πίεση]

he needs a blood transfusion khree*a*zete meta-ngheessee ematos [χρειάζεται μετάγγιση αἵματος]

bloody mary ena bloody mary [ἕνα μπλάντη Μαίρη]

blouse ee bloosa [ἡ μπλοῦζα]

» *TRAVEL TIP: blouse sizes*

UK:	32	34	36	38	40
Greece	42	44	46	48	50

blue ble [μπλέ]

board: full board pl*ee*rees theea-trof*ee* [πλήρης διατροφή]

half board eemee-theea-trof*ee* [ἡμιδιατροφή]

boarding pass thelt*ee*o epeeveevasseos [δελτεῖο ἐπιβιβάσεως]

boat to pl*ee*o [τό πλοῖο]

when is the next boat to . . .? pote *ee*ne to epomeno pl*ee*o ya . . .? [πότε εἶναι τό ἐπόμενο πλοῖο γιά . . .;]

body to soma [τό σῶμα]

(corpse) ena ptoma [ἕνα πτῶμα]

boil *(noun)* ena speeree [ἕνα σπυρί]

do we have to boil the water? khree*a*zete na vrasome to nero? [χρειάζεται νά βράζωμε τό νερό;]

boiled egg vrassto avgo [βραστό αὐγό]

bone ena kokalo [ἕνα κόκκαλο]

bonnet *(car)* to kapo [τό καπό]

book to veevleeo [τό βιβλίο]
   booking office to praktoreeo [τό πρακτορείο]
   can I book a seat for . . .? boro na kleesso
   meea thessee ya . . .? [μπορῶ νά κλίσω μιά θέση
   γιά . . .;]
bookshop ena vee-vlee-o-po-leeo [ἕνα
   βιβλιοπωλείο]
» *TRAVEL TIP: except for in the very expensive*
   restaurants it is not customary to book tables in
   Greece
boot ee bota [ή μπότα]
   (car) to port baghaz [τό πόρτ μπαγκάζ]
booze poto [ποτό]
   I had too much booze last night eepeea polee
   poto kh-thes to vrathee [ἤπια πολύ ποτό χθές τό
   βράδυ]
border to seenoro [τό σύνορο]
bored: I'm bored varee-e-me [βαριέμαι]
boring varetos [βαρετός]
born: I was born in . . . ye-neetheeka to . . .
   [γεννήθηκα τό . . .]
   see date
borrow: can I borrow . . .? boro na
   thaneessto? [μπορῶ νά δανειστῶ;]
boss to afendeeko [τό ἀφεντικό]
both: ke ee theeo [καί οἱ δύο]
   I'll take both of them tha paro ke ta theeo [θά
   πάρω καί τά δύο]
bottle ena bookalee [ἕνα μπουκάλι]
   bottle-opener to anee-kteeree [τό ἀνοικτήρι]
bottom: at the bottom of the hill stoos
   propothes too lofoo [στούς πρόποδες τοῦ λόφου]
bouncer o paleekaras [ό παλληκαράς]
bowels ta endera [τά ἔντερα]
bowl *(noun)* ena bol [ἕνα μπόλ]
box ena kootee [ἕνα κουτί]
boy to agoree [τό ἀγόρι]
boyfriend o feelos [ό φίλος]
bra to sootee-en [τό σουτιέν]
bracelet to vrakheeolee [τό βραχιόλι]

brakes ta frena [τά φρένα]
  could you check the brakes? boreete na elen-ksete ta frena? [μπορεῖτε νά ἐλέγξετε τά φρένα;]˙
  I had to brake suddenly eprepe na frenaro apotoma [ἔπρεπε νά φρενάρω ἀπότομα]
  he didn't brake then frenare [δέν φρέναρε]
brandy koneeak [κονιάκ]
bread to psomee [τό ψωμί]
  could we have some bread and butter? boroome na ekhome leego psomee ke leego vooteero? [μπορούμε νά ἔχομε λίγο ψωμί καί λίγο βούτυρο;]
  some more bread, please akomee leego psomee, parakalo [ἀκόμη λίγο ψωμί, παρακαλῶ]
break *(verb)* spazo [σπάζω]
  I think I've broken my arm nomeezo otee ekho spassee to kheree moo [νομίζω ὅτι ἔχω σπάσει τό χέρι μου]
breakable ef-*th*raf-sto [εὔθραυστο]
breakdown: I've had a breakdown khalase to aftokeeneeto moo [χάλασε τό αὐτοκίνητό μου]
  nervous breakdown nevreekos kloneesmos [νευρικός κλονισμός]
» *TRAVEL TIP: breakdown services; ring 104 for OVELPA* [ΟΒΕΛΠΑ]; *24 hour service from June 15–September 30; free service given to foreign motorists (except parts)*
breakfast to pro-ye-vma [τό πρόγευμα]
  English breakfast angleeko pro-ye-vma [᾽Αγγλικό πρόγευμα]
breast to steethos [τό στῆθος]
breath ee anapnoee [ἡ ἀναπνοή]
  he's getting very short of breath ekhee thees-pneea [ἔχει δύσπνοια]
breathe anapneo [ἀναπνέω]
  I can't breathe then boro na anapnefso [δέν μπορῶ νά ἀναπνεύσω]
bridge ee yefeera [ἡ γέφυρα]
briefcase o khartofeelakas [ὁ χαρτοφύλακας]

brighten up: do you think it'll brighten up later? nomeezete otee tha kaleeterepsee o keros argotera? [νομίζετε ὅτι θά καλλιτερέψει ὁ καιρός ἀργότερα;]

brilliant (*person*) tetraperatos [τετραπέρατος] (*idea, swimmer*) lambros [λαμπρός]

bring ferno [φέρνω]
could you bring it to my hotel? borees na to ferees sto ksenothokheeo moo? [μπορεῖς νά τό φέρεις στό ξενοδοχεῖο μου;]

Britain Vretaneea [Βρεταννία]

British Vretanos [Βρεταννός]

brochure ena feelatheeo [ἕνα φυλλάδιο]
have you got any brochures about . . . ? ekhete katholoo feelatheea ya . . . ? [ἔχετε καθόλου φυλλάδια γιά . . . ;]

broken spasmeno [σπασμένο]
you've broken it to espasses [τό ἔσπασες]
it's broken eene spasmeno [εἶναι σπασμένο]
my room/car has been broken into paraveeasan to thomateeo moo/aftokeeneeto moo [παραβίασαν τό δωμάτιό μου/αὐτοκίνητου]

brooch meea karfeetssa [μιά καρφίτσα]

brother: my brother o athelfos moo [ὁ 'ἀδελφός μου]

brown kafethee [καφεδί]
brown paper khartee pereeteeleegmatos [χαρτί περιτυλίγματος]
brown hair kastana maleea [καστανά μαλιά]

browse: can I just browse around? boro na reexo meea mateea yeero? [μπορῶ νά ρίξω μιά ματιά γύρω;]

bruise (*noun*) meea melaneea [μιά μελανιά]

brunette (*noun*) ee melakhreenee [ἡ μελαχρινή]

brush (*noun*) meea voortsa [μιά βοῦρτσα]

bucket o koovas [ὁ κουβᾶς]

buffet o boofes [ὁ μπουφές]

building to kteereeo [τό κτίριο]

bulb meea lampa [λάμπα]

the bulb's gone ee lampa ka-ee-ke [ἡ λάμπα κάικε]

bump: he's had a bump on the head kteepeesse to kefalee too [κτύπησε τό κεφάλι του]

bumper o pro-feelakteeras [ὁ προφυλακτήρας]

bunch of flowers ena booketo loolootheea [ἕνα μπουκέτο λουλούδια]

bunk meea kleenee [μιά κλίνη]

bunk beds koo-setes [κουσέτες]

buoy ee seemathoora [ἡ σημαδούρα]

burglar o kleftees [ὁ κλέφτης]

they've taken all my money klepsane ola moo ta lefta [κλέψανε ὅλα μου τά λεφτά]

burnt: this meat is burnt afto to kreas eene kameno [αὐτό τό κρέας εἶναι καμένο]

my arms are burnt ta khereea moo ka-ee-kane [τά χέρια μου καήκανε]

can you give me something for these burns? boreete na moo thossete katee yee-afta ta engha-vmata? [μπορεῖτε νά μου δώσετε κάτι γι᾽ αὐτά τά ἐγκαύματα;]

bus to leoforeeo [τό λεωφορεῖο]

bus stop ee stassee [ἡ στάση]

could you tell me when we get there? boreete na moo peete poo tha katevo? [μπορεῖτε νά μοῦ πῆτε ποῦ θά κατέβω;]

business: I'm here on business eeme etho ya thoolee-es [εἶμαι ἐδῶ γιά δουλειές]

business trip taxeethee ya thoolee-es [ταξίδι γιά δουλειές]

none of your business! then soo peftee logos [δέν σοῦ πέφτει λόγος]

bust to steethos [τό στῆθος]

» *TRAVEL TIP: bust measurements*

UK	32	34	36	38	40
Greece	80	87	91	97	102

busy *(telephone)* apa-skho-leemeno [ἀπασχολημένο]

are you busy? eeste apa-skho-leemenos?

[εἶστε ἀπασχολη't μένος;]

but ala [ἀλλά]
not this one but that one okhee afto ala
ekeeno [ὄχι αὐτό ἀλλά ἐκεῖνο]
butcher's o khasapees [ὁ χασάπης]
butter vooteero [βούτυρο]
button to koombee [τό κουμπί]
buy: I'll buy it tha to agorasso [θά τό ἀγοράσω]
where can I buy ...? poo boro n' agorasso?
[ποὺ μπορῶ ν' ἀγοράσω . . .;]
by: I'm here by myself eeme monos moo etho
[εἶμαι μόνος μου ἐδῶ]
are you by yourself? eese monos soo? [εἶσαι
μόνος σου;]
can you do it by tomorrow? borees na to
kanees mekhree avreeo? [μπορεῖς νά τό κάνεις
μέχρι αὔριο;]
by train/car/plane me treno/aftokeeneeto/
a-eroplano [μέ τραῖνο/αὐτοκίνητο/ἀεροπλάνο]
I parked by the trees parkara konda sta
thenthra [πάρκαρα κοντά στά δένδρα]
who's it made by? peeos to katasskevase?
[ποιός τό κατασκεύασε;]
cabaret to kabare [τό καμπαρέ]
cabbage ena lakhano [ἕνα λάχανο]
cabin *(on ship)* ee kabeena [ἡ καμπίνα]
cable *(noun)* to kalotheeo [τό καλώδιο]
café to zakharoplasteeo [τό ζαχαροπλαστεῖο]
» *TRAVEL TIP: cafés serve food and (alcoholic)*
drinks; in the cities they are usually open 24
hours a day; no problem with children
cake to 'cake' [τό κέϊκ]
a piece of cake ena komatee 'cake' [ἕνα κομάτι
κέϊκ]
calculator to ko-mpee-oo-terakee [τό
κομπιουτεράκι]
call fonazo [φωνάζω]
will you call the manager? fonazete ton
thee-ef-theendee? [φωνάζετε τόν διευθηντή;]
what is this called? pos to lene? [πῶς τό λένε;]

call box teelefoneek*os tha*lamos [τηλεφωνικός θάλαμος]

calm *(sea)* ee*r*emee [ἤρεμη]

calm down eer*e*meese [ἠρέμησε]

camera ee fotografeek*ee* meekhan*ee* [ἡ φωτογραφική μηχανή]

» *TRAVEL TIP: cameras in museums and archaeological sites usually permitted provided no tripod is used*

camp: is there somewhere we can camp? eep*a*rkhee m*e*ros na kataskeen*o*ssome? [ὑπάρχει μέρος νά κατασκηνώσωμε;]

can we camp here? bor*oo*me na kataskeen*o*ssome etho? [μπορούμε νά κατασκηνώσωμε ἐδῶ;]

camping holiday kataskee*e*nossee [κατασκήνωση]

campsite 'camping' [κάμπινγκ]

» *TRAVEL TIP: there is no free camping in Greece*

can¹: a can of beer mee*a* beera [μία μπύρα]

can-opener to aneekt*ee*ree [τό ἀνοικτήρι]

can²: can I have ...? boro na ekho ...? [μπορῶ νά ἔχω . . .;]

can you show me ...? bor*ee*te na moo thee*x*ete ...? [μπορεῖτε νά μοῦ δείξετε . . .;]

I can't ... then boro ... [δέν μπορῶ . . .]

he can't ... then bor*ee* [δέν μπορεῖ]

we can't ... then bor*oo*me [δέν μπορούμε]

Canada Kanath*a*s [Καναδάς]

Canadian Kanath*o*s [Καναδός]

cancel: I want to cancel my booking *the*lo na akeeroso tee *the*ssee moo [θέλω νά ἀκυρώσω τή θέση μου]

can we cancel dinner for tonight? bor*oo*me na akeer*o*some to fagee*to* ya seemera to vrath*ee*? [μπορούμε νά ἀκυρώσωμε τό φαγητό γιά σήμερα τό βράδυ;]

candle to ker*ee* [τό κερί]

capsize anapothogeer*ee*zo [ἀναποδογυρίζω]

car to aftok*ee*neeto [τό αὐτοκίνητο]

by car me aftok*ee*neeto [μέ αὐτοκίνητο]

carafe mee*a* karafa [μιά καράφα]

caravan trokho*spee*to [τροχόσπιτο]

carburettor to karbeerater [τό καρμπιρατέρ]

cards ee k*a*rtes [οἱ κάρτες]

do you play cards? pezete kharteea? [παίζετε χαρτιά]

care: goodbye, take care ad*ee*o ke na pros*se*khees [ἀντίο, καί νά προσέχεις]

will you take care of this suitcase for me? bor*ee*te na moo pros*e*xete af*tee* tee val*ee*dza [μπορεῖτε νά μου πρασέξετε αὐτή τή βαλίτσα]

careful: be careful pros*e*khe [πρόσεχε]

car-ferry to f*e*ree [τό φέρρυ]

car park to 'parking' [τό πάρκινγκ]

carpet to khal*ee* [τό χαλί]

carrot *e*na karoto [ἕνα καρόττο]

carry: will you carry this for me? bor*ee*te na moo seek*o*sete afto? [μπορεῖτε νά μου σηκώσετε αὐτό;]

carry-cot port-bebe [πόρτ-μπεμπέ]

carving ee gleeptee*kee* [ἡ γλυπτική]

case *(suitcase)* ee val*ee*dza [ἡ βαλίτσα]

cash metr*ee*ta [μετρητά]

I haven't any cash then *e*kho metr*ee*ta [δέν ἔχω μετρητά]

cash desk to tam*ee*o [τό ταμεῖο]

will you cash a cheque for me? bor*ee*te na moo exargeer*o*sete mee*a* epeetag*ee*? [μπορεῖτε νά μου ἐξαργυρώσετε μιά ἐπιταγή;]

casino to kaz*ee*no [τό καζίνο]

cassette kass*e*ta [κασσέτα]

cat ee g*a*ta [ἡ γάτα]

catch: where do we catch the bus? apo poo *tha* p*a*rome to le-ofor*ee*o? [ἀπό πού θά πάρωμε τό λεωφορεῖο;]

he's caught a bug kol*ee*sse mee*a* arost*ee*a [κόλλησε μιά ἀρρώστια]

cathedral o ka*th*ethreek*o*s naos [ὁ καθεδρικός ναός]

catholic *(adjective)* katholeeka [καθολικά]
cauliflower koonoopeethee [κουνουπίδι]
cave ee speeleea [ἡ σπηλιά]
ceiling to tavanee [τό ταβάνι]
celery seleeno [σέλινο]
cellophane selofan [σελοφάν]
centigrade Kelseeoo [Κελσίου]

» *TRAVEL TIP: to convert C to F:* $\frac{C}{5} \times 9 + 32 = F$

centigrade	−5	0	10	15	21	30	36.9
Fahrenheit	23	32	50	59	70	86	98.4

centimetre ekatossto [ἑκατοστό]
» *TRAVEL TIP: 1 cm = 0.39 inches*
central kendreekos [κεντρικός]
  with central heating me kendreek*ee*
  *the*rmansee [μέ κεντρική θέρμανση]
centre to kendro [τό κέντρο]
  how do we get to the centre? pos *th*a pame
  sto kendro tees pole-os? [πῶς θά πᾶμε στό κέντρο
  τῆς πόλεως;]
certain veve-os [βέβαιος]
  are you certain? *ee*se veve-os? [εἶσαι βέβαιος;]
certificate to peesto-pee-ee-teeko [τό
  πιστοποιητικό]
chain ee aleess*ee*tha [ἡ ἀλυσίδα]
chair ee karekla [ἡ καρέκλα]
chambermaid ee kamaree-*e*ra [ἡ καμαριέρα]
champagne sampaneea [σαμπάνια]
change: could you change this into
  drachmas? boreete na moo alaxete afto se
  thrakhm*e*s? [μπορεῖτε νά μοῦ ἀλλάξετε αὐτό σέ
  δραχμές;]
  I haven't any change then ekho pseela [δέν
  ἔχω ψιλά]
  do we have to change trains? prepee na
  alaxome treno? [πρέπει νά ἀλλάξωμε τραῖνο;]
  I'll just get changed *th*alaxo [θ' ἀλάξω]
» *TRAVEL TIP: changing money see* **bank**
channel: the Channel ee Mankhee [ἡ Μάγχη]
charge: what will you charge? posa *th*a

khreosete? [πόσα θά χρεώσετε;]
who's in charge? peeos eene eepefheenos?
[ποιός εἶναι ὑπεύθνος;]
chart o khartees [ό χάρτης]
cheap ftheenos [φθηνός]
have you got something cheaper? ekhete
teepote ftheenotero? [ἔχετε τίποτε φθηνότερο;]
cheat: I've been cheated moo tee skasane [μοῦ
τή σκάσανε]
check: will you check? boreete na elenxete?
[μπορεῖτε νά ἐλέγξετε;]
I'm sure, I've checked eeme vebe-os ekho
elenxee [εἶμαι βέβαιος, ἔχω ἐλέγξει]
will you check the total? boreete na elenxete
to logareeasmo? [μπορεῖτε νά ἐλέγξετε τό
λογαριασμό;]
cheek to magoolo [τό μάγουλο]
cheeky afthathees [αὐθάδης]
cheers (toast) steen eegeea soo [στήν ὑγειά σου]
(thank you) efkhareesto [εὐχαριστῶ]
cheerio (bye-bye) ya soo [γεία σου]
(toast) steen eegeea soo [στήν ὑγειά σου]
cheese to teeree [τό τυρί]
say cheese khamogelase [χαμογέλασε]
chef o chef [ό σέφ]
chemist's to farmakeeo [τό φαρμακεῖο]
cheque meea epeetegee [μιά ἐπιταγή]
will you take a cheque? pernete eppeetages?
[παίρνετε ἐπιταγές;]
cheque book veevleeo epeetagon [βιβλίο
ἐπιταγῶν]
» TRAVEL TIP: *paying by cheque is not standard
practice in Greece; only very big hotels, that have
their own bank, accept cheques; see* **bank**
chest to steethos [τό στῆθος]
» TRAVEL TIP: *chest measurements*

UK	34	36	38	40	42	44	46
Greece	87	91	97	102	107	112	117

chewing gum masteekha [μαστίχα]
chickenpox anemovlogeea [ἀνεμοβλογιά]

....

child to peth*ee* [τό παιδί]
  children ta pethe*ea* [τά παιδιά]
  children's portion petheek*ee* mere*e*tha
  [παιδική μερίδα]
» *TRAVEL TIP: only hotels giving full board or half*
  board serve children's portions; restaurants
  don't

chin to sagon*ee* [τό σαγόνι]
china porselan*ee* [πορσελάνη]
chips pat*a*tes teegane*ee*tes [πατάτες τηγανιτές]
  (casino) mark*e*s [μάρκες]
chocolate mee*a* sokol*a*ta [μιά σοκολάτα]
  hot chocolate mee*a* zest*ee* sokol*a*ta [μιά ζεστή
  σοκολάτα]
  a box of chocolates ena koot*ee* sokol*a*tes [ἕνα
  κουτί σοκολάτες]
choke *(car)* o a-*e*ras [ὁ ἀέρας]
chop *(noun)* mee*a* breez*o*la [μία μπριζόλα]
  pork/lamb chop kheereen*ee*/arn*ee*sseea
  breez*o*la [χοιρινή/ἀρνίσια μπριζόλα]
Christian name on*o*ma [ὄνομα]
Christmas khreest*oo*gena [Χριστούγεννα]
  happy Christmas! Kal*a* khreest*oo*gena!
  [Καλά Χριστούγεννα!]
church ee ekleess*ee*a [ἡ ἐκκλησία]
  where is the Protestant/Catholic Church?
  poo *ee*ne ee thee-amarteerom*e*nee/katholeek*ee*
  ekleess*ee*a? [ποῦ εἶναι ἡ διαμαρτυρόμενη/
  καθολική ἐκκλησία;]
cider meel*ee*tees [μηλίτης]
cigar to p*oo*ro [τό πούρο]
cigarette to tseeg*a*ro [τό τσιγάρο]
  would you like a cigarette? *the*lete ena
  tseeg*a*ro? [θέλετε ἕνα τσιγάρο;]
  tipped or plain me f*ee*ltro ee me khor*ee*s
  f*ee*ltro [μέ φίλτρο ἤ μέ χωρίς φίλτρο]
cine-camera ee keeneematografeek*ee*
  meekhan*ee* [ἡ κινηματογραφική μηχανή]
cinema to seen*e*ma [τό σινεμά]
circle o k*ee*klos [ὁ κύκλος]

(in cinema) ee plateea [ἡ πλατεῖα]

» *TRAVEL TIP: in Greek cinemas the circle is cheaper than the stalls*

city ee polee [ἡ πόλη]

claim *(insurance)* thee-ektheeko [διεκδικῶ]

clarify ksekathareezo [ξεκαθαρίζω]

clean *(adjective)* kathara [καθαρά]

can I have some clean sheets? boro na ekho kathara sedoneea? [μπορῶ νά ἔχω καθαρά σεντόνια;]

my room hasn't been cleaned today to thomateeo moo then kathareesteeke seemera [τό δωμάτιό μου δέν καθαρίστηκε σήμερα]

it's not clean then eene katharo [δέν εἶναι καθαρό]

cleansing cream galaktoma kathareesmoo [γαλάκτωμα καθαρισμοῦ]

clear: I'm not clear about it then eeme veve-os yee-afto [δέν εἶμαι βέβαιος γι' αὐτό]

clever exeepnos [ἔξυπνος]

climate to kleema [τό κλίμα]

» *TRAVEL TIP: one of the best Mediterranean climates; a short spring precedes a long, hot summer with temperatures up to 39°C and more; cooler on the islands; autumn, warmer than spring, followed by a mild winter; rain in summer unheard-of*

cloakroom gardaroba [γκαρνταρόμπα]

(WC) ee too-aleta [ἡ τουαλέτα]

clock to roloee [τό ρολόι]

close¹ konda [κοντά]

(weather) seenefeea [συννεφιά]

close²: when do you close? pote kleenete? [πότε κλείνετε;]

closed kleesto [κλειστό]

cloth to eefasma [τό ὕφασμα]

(rag) ena koorelee [ἕνα κουρέλι]

clothes ta rookha [τά ροῦχα]

cloud to seenefo [τό σύννεφο]

clutch to abra-ee-az [τό ἀμπραϊάζ]

the clutch is slipping to abra-ee-az pateenaree [τό ἀμπραιάζ πατηνάρει]

coach to poolman [τό πούλμαν]

coach party ee omatha too poolman [ἡ ὁμάδα τοῦ πούλμαν]

coast ee aktee [ἡ ἀκτή]

coastguard o aktofeelakas [ὁ ἀκτοφύλακας]

coat to palto [τό παλτό]

cockroach ee katsareetha [ἡ κατσαρίδα]

coffee o kafes [ὁ καφές]

a coffee, please ena kafe parakalo

YOU MAY THEN HEAR . . .

tee kafe? *what sort of coffee?*

eleeneeko kafe? *Greek coffee?*

nescafe? *instant coffee?*

me zakharee ee khorees zakharee? *with sugar or without sugar?*

» *TRAVEL TIP: Greek coffee is always black and strong with a lot of grounds at the bottom of the cup; if you'd like a white coffee ask for:* ena kafe me gala

coin to kerma [τό κέρμα]

cold kreeo [κρύο]

I'm cold kreeono [κρυώνω]

I've got a cold ekho kreeossee [ἔχω κρυώσει]

collapse: he's collapsed leepotheemeesse [λυποθύμησε]

collar to kolaro [τό κολλάρο]

» *TRAVEL TIP: collar sizes*

(old) UK:	14	14½	15	15½	16	16½	17
continental:	36	37	38	39	41	42	43

collect: I want to collect . . . thelo na mazepso . . . [θέλω νά μαζέψω . . .]

(pick up) thelo na paro . . . [θέλω νά πάρω . . .]

colour to khroma [τό χρῶμα]

have you any other colours? ekhete ala khromata? [ἔχετε ἄλλα χρώματα;]

comb ee khtena [ἡ χτένα]

come erkhome [ἔρχομαι]

I come from London erkhome apo to

Lontheeno [ἔρχομαι ἀπό τό Λονδίνο]
we came here yesterday *eerth*ame eth*o*
kth*thes* [εἴρθαμε ἐδῶ χθές]
come on! ela tora! [Ἔλα τώρα!]
come here ela eth*o* [Ἔλα ἐδῶ]
comfortable anapafteekos [ἀναπαυτικός]
it's not very comfortable then *eene* pol*ee*
anapafteek*o* [δέν εἶναι πολύ ἀναπαυτικό]
Common Market ee Keen*ee* Agor*a* [ἡ Κοινή
Ἀγορά]
communication cord s*ee*ma kinth*i*no [σῆμα
κινδύνου]
company *(business)* eter*ee*a [ἑταιρία]
you're good company *ees*e kal*ee* par*ea* [εἶσαι
καλή παρέα]
compartment *(train)* to theeamereesma [τό
διαμέρισμα]
compass ee peex*ee*tha [ἡ πυξίδα]
compensation ee apozeem*ee*-osee [ἡ
ἀποζημίωση]
I demand compensation apet*o*
apozeem*ee*-osee [ἀπαιτῶ ἀποζημίωση]
complain parapon*oo*me [παραπονοῦμαι]
**I want to complain about my room/the
waiter** *the*lo na parapon*etho* ya to thoma*tee*o
moo/to serveet*oro* [θέλω νά παραπονεθῶ γιά τό
δωμάτιό μου/τό σερβιτόρο]
have you got a complaints book? *e*khete
veevl*ee*o paraponon?
[ἔχετε βιβλίο παραπόνων;]
completely endel*os* [ἐντελῶς]
complicated: it's very complicated *ee*ne pol*ee*
per*ee*ploko [εἶναι πολύ περίπλοκο]
compliment: my compliments to the chef ta
seenkhareet*ee*re*ea* moo sto 'chef' [τά
συγχαρητήριά μου στό σέφ]
concert ee seenavl*ee*a [ἡ συναυλία]
concussion theeasseessee [διάσειση]
condition o or*os* [ὁ ὅρος]
it's not in very good condition then *ee*ne se

....

pol*ee* kal*ee* kat*a*stasee [δέν είναι σέ πολύ καλή κατάσταση]

conference to seemv*oo*leeo [τό συμβούλιο]

confession exomolog*ee*ssee [ἐξομολόγηση]

confirm: I want to confirm ... *the*lo na epeeveve-*o*sso ... [θέλω νά ἐπιβεβαιώσω ...]

confuse: you're confusing me me berth*e*vees [μέ μπερδεύεις]

congratulations! seenkhareet*ee*reea! [συγχαρητήρια!]

conjunctivitis fl*o*gosee too blef*a*roo [φλόγωση τοῦ βλεφάρου]

con-man apat*e*onas [ἀπατεώνας]

connection *(travel)* seenthessee [σύνδεση]

connoisseur eetheek*o*s [εἰδικός]

conscious: he is conscious *e*khee tees es*thee*ssees too [ἔχει τίς αἰσθήσεις του]

consciousness: he's lost consciousness *e*khase tees es*thee*ssees too [ἔχασε τίς αἰσθήσεις του]

constipation theeskeel*ee*otees [δυσκοιλιότης]

consul o pr*o*xenos [ὁ Πρόξενος]

consulate to proxen*ee*o [τό Προξενεῖο]

contact: how can I contact ...? pos boro na *e*rtho se epaf*ee* me ...? [πώς μπορῶ νά ἔρθω σέ ἐπαφή μέ ...;]

contact lenses fak*ee* epaf*ee*s [φακοί ἐπαφῆς]

contraceptive andee-seelee-pteek*o* [ἀντισυλληπτικό]

convenient voleek*o* [βολικό]

cook: the cook o ma*geeras* [ὁ μάγειρας]

it's not cooked then *ee*ne pseem*e*no [δέν είναι ψημένο]

it's beautifully cooked *ee*ne or*e*a pseem*e*no [εἶναι ὡραῖα ψημένο]

cooker ee kooz*ee*ma [ἡ κουζίνα]

cool throser*o* [δροσερό]

Corfu Kerk*ee*ra [Κέρκυρα]

corkscrew to aneekht*ee*ree [τό ἀνοικτήρι]

corn *(foot)* o ka*los* [ὁ κάλος]

....

corner ee gonee*a* [ἡ γωνιά]
  can we have a corner table? bor*oo*me na
  ekhome ena gonee-ako trapezee? [μπορούμε νά
  ἔχωμε ἕνα γωνιακό τραπέζι;]
cornflakes 'cornflakes' [κορν-φλέϊκς]
correct sost*os* [σωστός]
cosmetics kaleendeek*a* [καλλυντικά]
cost: what does it cost? p*o*sa kanee? [πόσα
  κάνει;]
  that's too much *ee*ne pola [εἶναι πολλά]
  I'll take it *th*a to par*o* [θά τό πάρω]
cotton wool to babak*ee* [τό μπαμπάκι]
couchette koos*se*ta [κουσέττα]
cough *(noun)* v*ee*kho [βήχω]
  cough syrup seerop*ee* ya to v*ee*kha [συρόπι
  γιά τό βήχα]
could: could you please ...? *th*a
  bor*oo*sate ...? [θά μπορούσατε ...;]
  could I have ...? bor*o* naekho ...? [μπορῶ νά
  ἔχω ...;]
country ee kh*o*ra [ἡ χώρα]
  in the country steen exokh*i* [στήν ἐξοχή]
couple: a couple of ... *(two)* ena zevgar*ee* ...
  [ἕνα ζευγάρι ...]
  (a few) mereek*a* [μερικά]
courier seenoth*os* [συνοδός]
course *(of meal)* pee-*a*to [πιάτο]
  of course nev*eos* [βεβαίως]
court: I'll take you to court *th*a se pao sto
  thekast*ee*ree*o* [θά σέ πάω στό δικαστήριο]
cousin: my cousin o exathelf*os* moo [ὁ
  ἐξάδελφός μου]
cover: keep him covered skepase ton [σκεπασέ
  τον]
  cover charge engh*ee*-eessee [ἐγγύηση]
cow ee agelath*a* [ἡ ἀγελάδα]
crab ena kavooree [ἕνα καβούρι]
crash: there's been a crash egeene ena
  trakareesm*a* [ἔγινε ἕνα τρακάρισμα]
  crash helmet to kran*os* [τό κράνος]

crazy trelos [τρελλός]
  you're crazy *ee*se trelos [εἶσαι τρελλός]
cream ka-eema*kee* [καϊμάκι]
  (for skin) krema therma*tos* [κρέμα δέρματος]
  (colour) khroma krem [χρῶμα κρέμ]
crêche pethee*kos* sta*thmos* [παιδικός σταθμός]
credit card *eth*nokarta [' Εθνοκάρτα]
Crete K*ree*tee [Κρήτη]
crisis kree*ss*ee [κρίση]
crisps tsseeps [τσίπς]
crossroads theeasta*v*rosee [διασταύρωση]
crowded yema*to ko*smo [γεμάτο κόσμο]
cruise ee kroo-a-zee-*er*a [ἡ κρουαζιέρα]
crutch *(for invalid)* to thekan*ee*kee [τό δεκανίκι]
cry: don't cry mee kles [μήν κλές]
cup to fleedza*nee* [τό φλιτζάνι]
  a cup of coffee *e*na fleedza*nee* kafe [ἔνα
  φλιτζάνι καφέ]
cupboard to ndoola*pee* [τό ντουλάπι]
curry ka*ree* [κάρι]
curtains ee koort*ee*na [ἡ κουρτίνα]
cushion to maxeela*ree* [τό μαξιλάρι]
Customs to telon*ee*o [τό τελωνεῖο]
» *TRAVEL TIP: it is illegal to take out of the country*
  stones etc you may have picked up from an
  ancient site
cut: I've cut myself kopeeka [κόπηκα]
cycle: can we cycle there? bor*oo*me na
  ka*no*me poth*ee*lato ek*ee*? [μποροῦμε νά κάνωμε
  ποδήλατο ἐκεῖ;]
cyclist o pothee*la*tees [ὁ ποδηλάτης]
cylinder o k*ee*leen-thros [ὁ κύλινδρος]
  cylinder-head gasket fla*dza* kapak*ee-oo*
  [φλάντζα καπακιοῦ]
Cyprus K*ee*pros [Κύπρος]
dad(dy): my dad(dy) o ba*bas*(baba*kas*) moo [ὁ
  μπαμπάς (μπαμπάκας) μου]
damage: I'll pay for the damage *tha* pleero*sso*
  ya tee zeem*ee*a [θά πληρώσω γιά τή ζημιά]
  damaged katastram*e*no [καταστραμένο]

damn! na paree ee orgee! [νά πάρει ἡ ὀργή!]

damp ee eegraseea [ἡ ὑγρασία]

dance: is there a dance on? ekhee khoro? [ἔχει χορό;]

   would you like to dance? thelete na khorepsete? [θέλετε νά χωρέψετε;]

dangerous epeekeentheenos [ἐπικίνδυνος]

dark skoteenos [σκοτεινός]

   when does it get dark? pote skoteenee-azee? [πότε σκοτεινιάζει;]

   dark blue ble skooro [μπλέ σκοῦρο]

darling agapee moo [ἀγάπη μου]

dashboard kadran aftokeeneetoo [καντράν αὐτοκινήτου]

date: what's the date? posses too meenos ekhome? [πόσες τοῦ μηνός ἔχομε;]

   can we make a date? boroome na kleessome ena randevoo? [μπορούμε νά κλείσωμε ἕνα ραντεβοῦ;]

   on the fifth of May stees pende Maeeoo [στίς πέντε Μαΐου]

   in 1951 to kheeleea eneakosseea peneenda ena [τό χίλια ἐννεακόσια πενήντα ἕνα]

   (fruit) khoormas [χουρμάς]

daughter: my daughter ee koree moo [ἡ κόρη μου]

day mera [μέρα]

dazzle: his lights were dazzling me ta fota too me teeflonane [τά φῶτα του μέ τυφλώνανε]

dead pethamenos [παθαμένος]

deaf koofos [κουφός]

deal: it's a deal seem-fonee-same [συμφωνήσαμε]

   will you deal with it? tha to kanoneessees? [θά τό κανονίσεις;]

dear *(expensive)* akreevo [ἀκριβό]

   Dear Sir agapeete Keeree-e [ἀγαπητέ Κύριε]

   Dear Madam agapeetee Keeree-a [ἀγαπητή Κυρία]

   Dear Nikos agapeete Neeko [ἀγαπητέ Νίκο]

December The*kem*vreeos [Δεκέμβριος]
deck kata*stroma* [κατάστρωμα]
   deckchair kare*kla* katastro*matos* [καρέκλα καταστρώματος]
declare: I have nothing to declare then e*kho* tee*pote* na thee*losso* [δέν ἔχω τίποτε νά δηλώσω]
deep va*thees* [βαθύς]
   is it deep? ee*ne* va*theea*? [εἶναι βαθιά;]
defendant o kateegoro*omenos* [ὁ κατηγορούμενος]
delay: the flight was delayed ee pteessee e*khe* kath*eess*tereessee [ἡ πτήση εἶχε καθυστέρηση]
deliberately epeeteethes [ἐπίτηδες]
delicate *(person)* leptos [λεπτός]
delicious ye-f*stee-kotatos* [γευστικώτατος]
delivery: is there another mail delivery? tha ksan*arth*ee o takhee-thromos? [θά ξανάρθει ὁ ταχυδρόμος;]
de luxe looks [λούξ]
democratic theemokrateekos [δημοκρατικός]
dent *(noun)* bathooloma [βαθούλωμα]
   you've dented my car moo tra*kares* to aftok*ee*neeto [μοῦ τράκαρες τό αὐτοκίνητο]
dentist othond*ee-atros* [ὀδοντίατρος]
   YOU MAY HEAR...
   aneexte to stoma sas *open wide*
   ksevga*lte* to stoma sas parakalo *please rinse out*
dentures ee massela [ἡ μασέλα]
deny: I deny it to arnoo*me* [τό ἀρνοῦμαι]
deodorant to aposmeeteeko [τό ἀποσμητικό]
departure anakho*reessee* [ἀναχώρηση]
depend: it depends (on ...) exartate [ἐξαρτάται]
deport apela*vno* [ἀπελαύνω]
deposit ee prokatavol*ee* [ἡ προκαταβολή]
   do I have to leave a deposit? prepee na thosso prokatavol*ee*? [πρέπει νά δώσω προκαταβολή;]
depressed th*leemenos* [θλιμμένος]
depth to vathos [τό βάθος]

desperate: I'm desperate for a drink petheno
ya ena poto [πεθαίνω γιά ἕνα ποτό]
dessert to epeethorpeeo [τό ἐπιδόρπιο]
destination o pro-oreesmos [ὁ προορισμός]
detergent to aporeepandeeko [τό ἀπορυπαντικό]
detour anangasteekee strofee [ἀναγκαστική
στροφή]
devalued eepoteemeemenos [ὑποτιμημένος]
develop: could you develop these? boreete na
tees emfaneessete? [μπορεῖτε νά τίς ἐμφανίσετε;]
diabetic theeaveeteekos [διαβητικός]
dialling code o kotheekos areethmos [ὁ κωδικός
ἀριθμός]
diamond to theeamandee [τό διαμάντι]
diarrhoea theeareea [διάρροια]
have you got something for diarrhoea?
ekhete katee ya tee theeareea? [ἔχετε κάτι γιά τή
διάρροια;]
diary to eemerologeeo [τό ἡμερολόγιο]
dictionary to lexeeko [τό λεξικό]
didn't *see* **not**
die petheno [πεθαίνω]
he's dying pethenee [πεθαίνει]
diesel *(fuel)* deezel [ντίζελ]
diet thee-eta [δίαιτα]
I'm on a diet eeme se thee-eta [εἶμαι σέ δίετα]
different: they are different eene
theeaforeteekee [εἶναι διαφορετικοί]
can I have a different room? boro na ekho
ena alo thomateeo? [μπορῶ νά ἔχω ἕνα ἄλλο
δωμάτιο;]
is there a different route? eeparkhee alos
thromos? [ὑπάρχει ἄλλος δρόμος;]
difficult theeskolos [δύσκολος]
digestion khonefssee [χώνευση]
dinghy to pleeareeo [τό πλοιάριο]
dining room ee trapezareea [ἡ τραπεζαρία]
dinner to theepno [τό δεῖπνο]
(midday) to ye-vma [τό γεῦμα]
dinner jacket smokeen [σμόκιν]

direct *(adjective)* kat ef*th*ean [κάτ' εὐθεῖαν]
  does it go direct? p*a*ee kat ef*th*ean? [πάει κάτ' εὐθεῖαν;]
dirty lerom*e*nos [λερωμένος]
disabled an*a*peeros [ἀνάπηρος]
disappear exafan*ee*zome [ἐξαφανίζομαι]
  it's just disappeared m*o*lees exafan*ee*steeke [μόλις ἐξαφανίστηκε]
disappointing apogo-ee-tefteek*o* [ἀπογοητευτικό]
disco deeskot*e*k [ντισκοτέκ]
  see you in the disco *th*a se tho stee deeskot*e*k [θά σέ δῶ στή ντισκοτέκ]
discount ekpt*o*see [ἔκπτωση]
disgusting seekham*e*no [συχαμένο]
dish *(food)* pee*a*to [πιάτο]
dishonest then e*e*ne te*e*meeos [δέν εἶναι τίμιος]
disinfectant to apoleemandeek*o* [τό ἀπολυμαντικό]
dispensing chemist to farmak*ee*o [τό φαρμακεῖο]
distance ee apost*a*see [ἡ ἀπόσταση]
distilled water apostagm*e*no ner*o* [ἀποσταγμένο νερό]
distress signal s*e*ema keenth*ee*noo [σῆμα κινδύνου]
distributor *(car)* deestreebeet*e*r [ντιστριμπυτέρ]
disturb: the noise is disturbing us o*th*oreevos mas enokhl*ee* [ὁ θόρυβος μᾶς ἐνοχλεῖ]
divorced khoreesm*e*nos [χωρισμένος]
do: how do you do? kh*e*ro pol*e*e [χαίρω πολύ]
  what are you doing tonight? tee k*a*nete s*e*emera to vr*a*thee? [τί κάνετε σήμερα τό βράδυ;]
  how do you do it? pos to k*a*nete? [πῶς τό κάνετε;]
  will you do it for me? bor*e*ete na moo to k*a*nete? [μπορεῖτε νά μοῦ τό κάνετε;]
  I've never done it before then to *e*kho ksanak*a*nee [δέν τό ἔχω ξανακάνει]

I was doing 60 kph etrekha exeenda
heeleeometra [ἔτρεχα ἑξήντα χιλιόμετρα]

doctor o ya-tros [ὁ γιατρός]

I need a doctor khree-azome ena ya-tro
[χρειάζομαι ἕνα γιατρό]

» *TRAVEL TIP: free emergency treatment is provided
by first-aid centres; dial 100 and ask for an
ambulance*

YOU MAY HEAR ...

tokhete ksanapathee? *have you had this before?*

poo ponaee? *where does it hurt?*

pernete kanena farmako? *are you taking any
drugs?*

parte ena/theeo apo afta *take one/two of these*
**kathe trees ores/kathe mera/theeo fores teen
eemera** *every three hours/every day/twice a day*

document to engrafo [τό ἔγγραφο]

dog o skeelos [ὁ σκύλος]

don't! mee! [μή!] *see* **not**

door ee porta [ἡ πόρτα]

dosage ee thossee [ἡ δόση]

double: double room ena theeplo thomateeo
[ἕνα διπλό δωμάτιο]

double whisky ena theeplo 'whisky' [ἕνα
διπλό οὐΐσκι]

down: down the road para kato [πάρα κάτω]

downstairs kato [κάτω]

get down! kateva kato [κατέβα κάτω]

drain *(noun)* o okhetos [ὁ ὀχετός]

drawing pin meea peeneza [μιά πινέζα]

dress to foostanee [τό φουστάνι]

dressing gown ee roba [ἡ ρόμπα]

» *TRAVEL TIP: dress sizes*

UK	10	12	14	16	18	20
Greece	36	38	40	42	44	46

dressing *(for wound)* gaza [γάζα]
(for salad) latholemono [λαδολέμονο]

drink ena poto [ἕνα ποτό]

would you like a drink? thelete ena poto?
[θέλετε ἕνα ποτό;]

I don't drink then p**ee**no [δέν πίνω]
is the water drinkable? to nero **ee**ne
pos**ee**mo? [τό νερό εἶναι πόσιμο;]
drive: I've been driving all day othee**goo**ssa
olee mera [ὁδηγούσα ὅλη μέρα]
driver o othee**gos** [ὁ ὁδηγός]
driving license atheea othee**gee**sseos [ἄδεια
ὁδηγήσεως]

» TRAVEL TIP: driving in Greece: 100 kph is the
maximum speed; see also breakdowns,
roundabout

drown: he's drowning pn**ee**gete [πνίγεται]
drug farmako [φάρμακο]
drunk (adjective) meth**ee**smenos [μεθυσμένος]
dry steg**nos** [στεγνός]
  dry-cleaner's stegnokath**aree**sstee-reeo
  [στεγνοκαθαριστήριο]
due: when is the bus due? pote thar**thee** to
leoforeeo? [πότε θἄρθει τό λεωφορεῖο;]
during kata tee thee**ar**keea [κατά τή διάρκεια]
dust sk**o**nee [σκόνη]
duty-free aforolog**ee**to [ἀφορολόγητο]
dynamo to theenamo [τό δυναμό]
each: can we have one each? bop**oo**me na
ekhomee mee**a** o k**a**thenas? [μπορούμε νά ἔχομε ἕνα
ὁ καθένας;]
  how much are they each? poso ekhee to
k**a**thena? [πόσο ἔχει τό κάθε ἕνα;]
ear to af**tee** [τό αὐτί] I have earache pon**a**ee to
af**tee** moo [πονάει τό αὐτί μου]
early nor**ees** [νωρίς]
  we want to leave a day earlier **the**lome na
feegome mee**a** mera nor**ee**tera [θέλομε νά
φύγωμε μιά μέρα νωρίτερα]
earring to skoolar**ee**kee [τό σκουλαρίκι]
east ee anatol**ee** [ἡ ἀνατολή]
Easter o Pas-kha [τό Πάσχα]
easy efkolos [εὔκολος]
eat trogo [τρώγω]
  something to eat katee na fa-o [κάτι νά φάω]

egg ena avgo [ἕνα αὐγό]
Eire Noteeos Eerlantheea [Νότιος 'Ιρλανδία]
either: either ... or ... ee ... ee ...
[ἤ ... ἤ ...]
  I don't like either then maresee oote to ena
  oote to alo
  [δέν μάρέσει οὔτε τό ἕνα οὔτε τό ἄλλο]
elastic elasteekos [ἐλαστικός]
  elastic band lasteekho [λάστιχο]
elbow o anghonas [ὁ ἀγκώνας]
electric eelektreekos [ἠλεκτρικός]
  electric fire ee eelektreekee somba
  [ἡ ἠλεκτρική σόμπα]
electrician o eelektrologos [ὁ ἠλεκτρολόγος]
elegant kompsos [κομψός]
electricity eelektreesmos [ἠλεκτρισμός]
else: something else katee alo [κάτι ἄλλο]
  somewhere else kapoo aloo [κάπου ἀλλοῦ]
  who else? p-yee alee? [ποιοί ἄλλοι;]
  or else eethalos [εἰδάλως]
embarrassed eene se ameekhaneea [εἶναι σέ
  ἀμηχανία]
embarrassing fernee se ameekhaneea [φέρνει
  σέ ἀμηχανία]
embassy ee Presveea [ἡ Πρεσβεία]
emergency epeegoossa ananghee [ἐπείγουσα
  ἀνάγκη]
empty atheeanos [ἀδειανός]
enclose: I enclose ... essokleeo [ἐσωκλείω]
end telos [τέλος]
  when does it end? pote teleeonee? [πότε
  τελειώνει;]
engaged *(telephone, toilet)* apaskholeemeno
  [ἀπασχολημένο]
  (person) aravoneeasmenos [ἀρραβωνιασμένος]
engagement ring ee vera [ἡ βέρρα]
engine ee meekhanee [ἡ μηχανή]
  engine trouble meekhaneeko provleema
  [μηχανικό πρόβλημα]
England Angleea ['Αγγλία]

English Anglos ['Αγγλος]

enjoy: I enjoyed it very much mooaresse para polee [μοῦ ἄρεσε πάρα πολύ]

enlargement *(photo)* megentheessee [μεγένθυση]

enormous terassteeos [τεράστιος]

enough: thank you, that's enough efkhareesto, ftanee [εὐχαριστῶ, φτάνει]

entertainment ee theeaskethassee [ἡ διασκέδαση]

entrance ee eessothos [ἡ εἴσοδος]

envelope o fakelos [ὁ φάκελλος]

equipment ergaleea [ἐργαλεῖα]

error lathos [λάθος]

escalator ee keeleeomenee skala [ἡ κυλιώμενη σκάλα]

especially keereeos [κυρίως]

essential vasseekos [βασικός]
it is essential that ... eene vasseeko na ... [εἶναι βασικό νά ...]

Europe ee Evropee [ἡ Εὐρώπη]

evacuate atheeazo [ἀδειάζω]

even: even the British akomee ke ee Vretanee [ἀκόμη καί οἱ Βρεταννοί]

evening to theeleeno [τό δειλινό]
this evening seemera to apoyevma [σήμερα τό ἀπόγευμα]
good evening kaleespera [καλησπέρα]
evening dress vratheeno forema [βραδυνό φόρεμα]

ever: have you ever been to ...? ekhete paee pote ...? [ἔχετε πάει ποτέ ...;]

every kathe [κάθε]
every day kathe mera [κάθε μέρα]
everyone kathenas [καθένας]
everything ola [ὅλα]
everywhere pandoo [παντοῦ]

evidence meea apotheexee [μιά ἀπόδειξη]

exact akreevees [ἀκριβής]

example to paratheegma [τό παράδειγμα]

for example paratheegmatos kharee
[παραδείγματος χάρη]
excellent exokhos [ἔξοχος]
except ektos [ἐκτός]
   except me ektos apo mena [ἐκτός ἀπό μένα]
excess eepervolee [ὑπερβολή]
   excess baggage eepervaro [ὑπέρβαρο]
exchange *(money)* to seenalagma [τό
συνάλλαγμα]
   (telephone) teelefoneekee seentheealexee
[τηλεφωνική συνδιάλεξη]
exciting seenarpasteekos [συναρπαστικός]
excursion meea ekthromee [μιά ἐκδρομή]
excuse me *(to get past etc)* me seenkhoreete [μέ
συγχωρεῖτε]
   (to get attention) sas parakalo [σᾶς παρακαλῶ]
   (apology) me seenkhoreete [μέ συγχωρεῖτε]
exhaust *(car)* ee exatmeessee [ἡ ἐξάτμιση]
exhausted exandleemenos [ἐξαντλημένος]
exit ee exothos [ἡ ἔξοδος]
expect: she's expecting eene se
entheeaferoossa [εἶναι σέ ἐνδιαφέρουσα]
expenses: it's on expenses pereelamvanlete
sta exotha [περιλαμβάνεται στά ἔξοδα]
expensive akreevo [ἀκριβό]
   that's too expensive afto eene polee akreevo
[αὐτό εἶναι πολύ ἀκριβό]
expert eetheekos [εἰδικός]
explain exeego [ἐξηγῶ]
   would you explain that slowly? boreete na
to exeegeessete afto arga? [μπορεῖτε νά τό
ἐξηγήσετε αὐτό ἀργά;]
export *(noun)* exagogee [ἐξαγωγή]
exposure meter to fotometro [τό φωτόμετρο]
extra extra [ἔξτρα]
   an extra glass/day ena poteeree extra/meea
mera extra [ἕνα ποτήρι ἔξτρα/μιά μέρα ἔξτρα]
   is that extra? ekeeno eene extra? [ἐκεῖνο εἶναι
ἔξτρα;]
extremely eepervoleeka [ὑπερβολικά]

....

eye to ma**tee** [τό μάτι]
  eyebrow to free**thee** [τό φρύδι]
  eyeshadow skee*a* ma**tee**-*oo* [σκιά ματιού]
  eye witness o af**top**tees ma**rtees** [ό αὐτόπτης
  μάρτης]
face to pro**ssopo** [τό πρόσωπο]
  face mask *(diving)* ee ma**ska** [ή μάσκα]
fact ye**gonos** [γεγονός]
factory to ergo**stasseo** [τό ἐργοστάσιο]
Fahrenheit Fahrenheit [Φαρενάϊτ]

» *TRAVEL TIP: to convert F to C: $F - 32 \times \dfrac{5}{9} = C$*

Fahrenheit	32	50	59	70	86	98.4
centigrade	0	10	15	21	30	36.9

faint: she's fainted leepo*thee*meesse
  [λιποθύμησε]
fair *(fun-)* to panee**gee**ree [τό πανηγύρι]
  (commercial) ee ek-*th*essee [ή ἔκθεση]
  that's not fair then ee*ne* the**eko** [δέν εἴναι
  δίκαιο]
faithfully: yours faithfully eeleekreen*a*
  theek*os* sas [εἰλικρινά δικός σας]
fake pla**sto** [πλαστό]
fall: he's fallen *e*pesse [ἔπεσε]
false psef**teekos** [ψεύτικος]
family ee eekoge**neea** [ή οἰκογένεια]
fan *(cooling)* o anemees**tee**ras [ό ἀνεμιστήρας]
  (hand-held) ee venta**leea** [ή βεντάλια]
  fan belt loo*ree* anemees**teera** [λουρί
  ἀνεμιστήρα]
far ma**kreea** [μακρυά]
  is it far? ee*ne* ma**kreea?** [εἴναι μακρυά;]
  how far is it? posso ma**kreea** ee*ne*? [πόσο
  μακριά εἴναι;]
fare *(travel)* ta na**vla** [τά ναῦλα]
farm to agrok**teema** [τό ἀγρόκτημα]
farther pee*o* ma**kreea** [πιό μακρυά]
fashion ee mo**tha** [ή μόδα]
fast gree**gora** [γρήγορα]
  don't speak so fast m*ee* mee*las* tosso gree**gora**

[μή μιλᾶς τόσο γρήγορα]

fat *(adjective, noun)* khonthros [χοντρός]

fatally *th*anasseema [θανάσιμα]

father: my father o pateras moo [ὁ πατέρας μου]

fathom or-ya [ὀργυιά]

fault vlavee [βλάβη]

  it's not my fault then fte-o ego [δέν φταίω ἐγώ]

faulty elatomateeko [²λαττωματικό]

favourite *(adjective)* agapeemeno [ἀγαπημένο]

February Fevrooareeos [Φεβρουάριος]

fed-up: I'm fed-up eeme varee-esteemenos [εἶμαι βαριεστημένος]

feel: I feel cold/hot/sad kreeono/zestenome/ eeme leepeemenos [κρυώνω/ζεσταίνομαι/εἶμαι λυπημένος]

  I feel like . . . *th*a eetha ela [θά ἤθελα]

ferry to ferry-boat [τό φέρρυμποτ]

fetch: will you come and fetch me? *th*art*h*ees na me parees? [θἄρθεις νά μέ πάρεις;]

fever o peeretos [ὁ πυρετός]

few: only a few mono leegee [μόνο λίγοι]

  a few days leeges meres [λίγες μέρες]

fiancé(e) o aravoneeasteekos/ee aravoneeasteekeea [ὁ ἀρραβωνιαστικός/ἡ ἀρραβωνιαστικιά]

fiddle: it's a fiddle eene apatee [εἶναι ἀπάτη]

field to khorafee [τό χωράφι]

fifty-fifty meessa-meessa [μισά-μισά]

figs seeka [σῦκα]

figure *(number)* o areethmos [ἀριθμός]

  (of person) ee seeloo-eta [ἡ σιλουέττα]

  I'm watching my figure prosekho tee seeloo-eta moo [προσέχω τή σιλουέττα μου]

fill: fill her up gemeesse to [γέμισέ το]

  to fill in a form gemeezo meea forma [γεμίζω μιά φόρμα]

fillet to feeleto [τό φιλέτο]

film to film [τό φίλμ]; **do you have this type of film?** ekhete teteeo film? [ἔχετε τέτοιο φίλμ;]

filter *(traffic)* feeltro [φίλτρο]
filter or non-filter? me feeltro ee mee khorees feeltro? [μέ φίλτρο ἤ μέ χωρίς φίλτρο;]
find vreesko [βρίσκω]
if you find it . . . an to vrees [ἄν τό βρεῖς]
I've found a . . . vreeka ena . . . [βρῆκα ἕνα . . .]
fine *(weather)* ore-os [ὡραῖος]
a 500 drachma fine pendakossee-es threkhmes prosteemo [500 δραχμές πρόστιμο]
OK, that's fine endaxee, seemfono [ἐντάξη, συμφωνῶ]
finger to thakteelo [τό δάκτυλο]
fingernail to neekhee [τό νύχι]
finish: I haven't finished then teleeossa [δέν τελείωσα]
fire: fire! foteea! [φωτιά!]
can we light a fire here? boroome na anapsome meea foteea etho? [μπορούμε νά ἀνάψωμε μιά φωτιά ἐδῶ;]
it's not firing *(car)* then ksekeena-ee [δέν ξεκινάει]
fire brigade peerosvesteekee [πυροσβεστική]
fire extinguisher o peerosvesteeras [ὁ πυροσβεστήρας]
» *TRAVEL TIP: dial 199 or 100*
first protos [πρῶτος]
I was first eemoona protos [ἤμουνα πρῶτος]
first aid protes voeethee-es [πρῶτες βοήθειες]
first aid kit efotheea proton voeetheeon [ἐφόδια πρῶτων βοηθειῶν]
first name onoma [ὄνομα]
first class *(travel etc)* protee thessee [πρώτη θέση]
fish to psaree [τό ψάρι]
fix: can you fix it? *(arrange, repair)* borees na to theeorthossees? [μπορεῖς νά τό διορθώσεις;]
fizzy me anthrakeeko [μέ ἀνθρακικό]
flag ee seemea [ἡ σημαία]
flash *(photography)* to flash [τό φλάς]

flat *(adjective)* ep*ee*petho [ἐπίπεδο]
  this drink is flat aft*o* to pot*o* *ee*ne
  ks*eth*eemasmeno [αὐτό τό ποτό εἶναι
  ξεθυμασμένο]
  I've got a flat (tyre) m*e*peeasse l*a*ssteekho
  [μ 'ἔπιασε λάστιχο]
  (apartment) to theeam*e*reesma [τό διαμέρισμα]
flavour ee ye-fssee [ἡ γεύση]
flea *e*nas ps*ee*los [ἕνας ψύλλος]
flies *(trousers)* to fermoo*a*r [τό φερμουάρ]
flight ee pt*ee*ssee [ἡ πτήση]
flippers ta vatrakhop*e*theela [τά
  βατραχοπέδιλα]
flirt *(verb)* flert*a*ro [φλερτάρω]
float *(verb)* epe*e*ple*o* [ἐπιπλέω]
floor to p*a*toma [τό πάτωμα]
  on the second floor sto th*e*ftero p*a*toma [στό
  δεύτερο πάτωμα]
flower to looloothee [τό λουλούδι]
flu gr*ee*pee [γρίππη]
fly *(insect)* m*ee*a m*ee*ga [μιά μύγα]
foggy omeekhlothees [ὀμιχλώδης]
follow akoloo*tho* [ἀκολουθῶ]
food to fageet*o* [τό φαγητό]
  food poisoning trofik*ee* theel*ee*teer*ee*assee
  [τροφική δηλητηρίαση]
fool anoeetos [ἀνόητος]
foot to pothee [τό πόδι]
» *TRAVEL TIP: 1 foot = 30.1 cm = 0.3 metres*
football *(game)* poth*o*ssfero [ποδόσφαιρο]
for ya [γιά]
forbidden apagorevmeno [ἀπαγορευμένο]
foreign kseno [ξένο]
  foreign exchange ks*e*no seen*a*lagma [ξένο
  συνάλλαγμα]
foreigner ks*e*nos [ξένος]
forget: I forget ksekhn*o* [ξεχνῶ]
  I've forgotten kse-kha-ssa [ξέχασα]
  don't forget mee kse-kha-ssees
  [μή ξεχάσεις]

I'll never forget you then *th*a se kse-kha-sso pote [δέν θά σέ ξεχάσω ποτέ]

fork ena peeroonee [ἕνα πηρούνι]

form *(document)* ee forma [ἡ φόρμα]

formal epeesseemo [ἐπίσημο]

fortnight theeo evthomathes [δυό ἑβδομάδες]

forward *(adverb)* brossta [μπροστά]

   forwarding address thee-*ef*theenssee apostolees [διεύθυνση ἀποστολῆς]

   could you forward my mail? boreete na moo steelete ta gramata moo? [μπορεῖτε νά μοῦ στίλετε τά γράμματά μου;]

fracture katagma [κάταγμα]

fragile ef-*th*rafsto [εὔθραυστο]

fraud apatee [ἀπάτη]

free eleftheros [ἐλεύθερος]

   admission free eleftera eessothos [ἐλευθέρα εἴσοδος]

freight forteeo [φορτίο]

freshen up: I want to freshen up *the*lo na freskareesto [θέλω νά φρεσκαριστῶ]

Friday Paraskevee [Παρασκευή]

fridge to pseegeeo [τό ψυγεῖο]

friend o feelos [ὁ φίλος]

friendly feeleeka [φιλικά]

from apo [ἀπό]

   where is it from? apo poo eene? [ἀπό ποῦ εἶναι;]

front *(noun)* brossta [μπροστά]

   in front of you brossta soo [μπροστά σου]

   in the front brossta [μπροστά]

frost pagoneea [παγωνιά]

frozen pagomenos [παγωμένος]

fruit frooto [φροῦτο]

fry teeganeezo [τηγανίζω]

   nothing fried teepote teeganeeto [τίποτε τηγανιτό]

   fried egg avgo teeganeeto [αὐγό τηγανιτό]

   frying pan to teeganee [τό τηγάνι]

fuel ta kafsseema [τά καύσιμα]

full gematos [γεμάτος]

fun: it's fun *ee*ne theeaskethasteeko [εἶναι διασκεδαστικό]

funny *(strange)* peree-ergo [περίεργο]
(comical) assteeo [ἀστεῖο]

furniture ta *e*peepla [τά ἔπιπλα]

further parapera [παραπέρα]

fuse ee asf*a*leea [ἡ ἀσφάλεια]

fuss fassareea [φασαρία]

future to m*e*lon [τό μέλλον]
in future sto m*e*lon [στό μέλλον]

gale *thee*-ela [θύελλα]

gallon ena gal*o*nee [ἕνα γαλόνι]
» *TRAVEL TIP: 1 gallon = 4.55 litres*

gallstone petra tees khol*ee*s [πέτρα τῆς χολῆς]

gamble khartopezo [χαρτοπαίζω]

gammon zambon [ζαμπόν]

garage *(repair)* to seenergeeo [τό συνεργεῖο]
(petrol) ee venz*ee*nee [ἡ βενζίνη]
(parking) to garaz [τό γκαράζ]

garden o k*ee*pos [ὁ κῆπος]

garlic skortho [σκόρδο]

gas to fota-ereeo [τό φωταέριο]
(petrol) to gazee [τό γκάζι]
gas cylinder meea fee-*a*lee a-ereeoo [μιά φιάλη ἀερίου]

gasket ee fl*a*ndza [ἡ φλάντζα]

gay *(homosexual)* tee-ootos [τοιοῦτος]

gear *(car)* ee takh*ee*teeta [ἡ ταχύτητα]
(equipment) erg*a*leea [ἐργαλεῖα]
gearbox trouble khalasm*e*no sasm*a*n [χαλασμένο σασμάν]
gear lever levg*e*s takhee*tee*ton [λεβγές ταχυτήτων]
I can't get it into gear then boro na v*a*lo takhee*tee*ta [δέν μπορῶ νά βάλω ταχύτητα]

gents anthron [ἀνδρῶν]

gesture kheeronom*e*ea [χειρονομία]
» *TRAVEL TIP: an outstretched open palm is a rude gesture in Greece*

get: will you get me a . . .? moo ferneteena . . .?
[μοῦ φέρνετε ἕνα . . .;]

how do I get to the ferry? pos boro na pao sto
ferry? [πῶς μπορῶ νά πάω στό φέρυ;]

when can I get it back? pote bopo na to paro
peesso? [πότε μπορῶ νά τό πάρω πίσω;]

when do we get back? pote yeereezome?
[πότε γυρίζωμε;]

where do I get off? poo katevenome? [ποῦ
κατεβαίνομε;]

where do I get a bus for . . .? apo poo
pernome to leoforeeo ya . . .? [ἀπό ποῦ πέρνομε
τό λεωφορεῖο γιά . . .;]

have you got . . .? ekhete . . .? [ἔχετε . . .;]

gin gin [τζίν]

gin and tonic gin me tonic [τζίν μέ τόνικ]

ginger ale ginger ale [τζιντζερέιλ]

girl ena koreetssee [ἕνα κορίτσι]

my girlfriend ee feelenatha moo [ἡ φιλενάδα
μου]

give theeno [δίνω]

will you give me . . .? moo theenete? [μοῦ
δίνετε;]

I gave it to him too tothossa [τοῦ τόδωσα]

glad efkhareesteemenos [εὐχαριστημένος]

glandular fever atheneekos peeretos [ἀδενικός
πυρετός]

glass to ya-lee [τό γυαλί]

(drinking) ena poteeree [ἕνα ποτήτι]

a glass of water ena poteeree nero [ἕνα ποτήρι
νερό]

glasses ta ya-leea [τά γυαλιά]

glue ee kola [ἡ κόλλα]

go: can I have a go? boro na prosspatheesso?
[μπορῶ νά προσπαθήσω;]

my car won't go to aftokeeneeto moo then
ksekeenaee [τό αὐτοκίνητό μου δέν ξεκινάει]

when does the bus go? pote tha feegee to
leoforeeo? [πότε θά φύγει τό λεωφορεῖο;]

it/he's gone efeege [ἔφυγε]

I want to go to Delphi the lo na pao stoos
Thelfoos [θέλω νά πάω στούς Δελφούς]
I want to go thelo na feego [θέλω νά φύγω]
goal goal [γκόλ]
goat ee katseeka [ή κατσίκα]
  goat's cheese teeree apo katseeka [τυρί ἀπό
  κατσίκα]
God o Theos [ό Θεός]
goddess ee thea [ή Θεά]
gold o khreessos [ό χρυσός]
golf to golf [τό γκόλφ]
good kala [καλά]
  good! kala! [καλά!]
goodbye ya soo [γειά σου]
gooseberries frangosstafeela
  [φραγκοστάφυλλα]
gramme to gramareeo [τό γραμμάριο]
» *TRAVEL TIP: 100 grammes = approx 3½ oz*
grand exokhos [ἔξοχος]
  granddaughter ee engonee [ή ἐγγονή]
  grandfather o papoos [ό παππούς]
  grandmother ee ya-ya [ή γιαγιά]
  grandson o engonos [ό ἐγγονός]
grapes stafeeleea [σταφύλια]
  grapefruit grapefruit [γκρέϊπφρουτ]
  grapefruit juice kheemos apo grapefruit
  [χυμός ἀπό γκρέϊπφρουτ]
grass to khortaree [τό χορτάρι]
grateful evgnomon [εὐγνώμων]
  I'm very grateful to you saseeme evgnomon
  [σᾶς εἶμαι εὐγνώμων]
gratitude evgnomosseenee [εὐγνωμοσύνη]
gravy ee saltssa [ή σάλτσα]
grease to grasso [τό γράσο]
greasy leeparos [λιπαρός]
great megalos [μεγάλος]
  great! thavmasseea! [θαυμάσια!]
Greece Elas [Ἑλλάς]
  in Ancient Greece steen Arkhea Elatha [στήν
  Ἀρχαῖα Ἑλλάδα]

Greek Eleenas [Ἕλληνας]
 I don't speak Greek then meelo Eleeneeka
 [δέν μιλῶ Ἑλληνικά]
 the Greeks ee Eleenes [οἱ Ἕλληνες]
greedy akhortagos [ἀχόρταγος]
green prasseeno [πράσινο]
 greengrocer's o manavees [ὁ μανάβης]
grey greezos [γκρίζος]
grocer's o bakalees [ὁ μπακάλης]
ground to ethafos [τό ἔδαφος]
 on the ground sto ethafos [στό ἔδαφος]
 on the ground floor sto eessogeeo [στό
 ἰσόγειο]
group ee omatha [ἡ ὁμάδα]
 our group leader o arkheegos tees omathas
 mas [ὁ ἀρχηγός τῆς ὁμάδας μας]
 I'm with the English group eeme me teen
 Angleekee omatha [εἶμαι μέ τήν 'Αγγλική
 ὁμάδα]
guarantee engee-eessee [ἐγγύηση]
 is there a guarantee? eeparkhee
 engee-eessee? [ὑπάρχει ἐγγύηση;]
guest o feelexenoomenos [ὁ φιλοξενούμενος]
guesthouse ee pansseeon [ἡ πανσιόν]
guide o ksenagos [ὁ ξεναγός]
guilty o enokhos [ὁ ἔνοχος]
guitar ee keethara [ἡ κιθάρα]
gum *(in mouth)* to oolo [τό οὖλο]
gun to oplo [τό ὅπλο]
gynaecologist o geenekologos [ὁ γυναικολόγος]
hair ta maleea [τά μαλλιά]
 hairbrush ee voortssa [ἡ βοὖρτσα]
 where can I get a haircut? poo boro na kopso
 ta maleea moo? [ποῦ μπορῶ νά κόψω τά μαλιά
 μου;]
 is there a hairdresser's here? eeparkhee
 komoteereeo etho? [ὑπάρχει κομμωτήριο ἐδῶ;]
 hair grip peeastrakee maleeon [πιαστράκι
 μαλλιῶν]
half meessos [μισός]

a half portion meess*ee* mer*ee*tha [μισή μερίδα]
half an hour meess*ee* *o*ra [μισή ώρα]
ham kheer*ee*n*o* [χοιρινό]
  hamburger h*a*mburger [χάμπουργκερ]
hammer *e*na sfeer*ee* [ένα σφυρί]
hand to kh*e*ree [τό χέρι]
  handbag ee ts*a*nda [ή τσάντα]
  handbrake kheer*o*freno [τό χειρόφρενο]
  handkerchief to mand*ee*lee [τό μαντήλι]
  handle to kher*oo*lee [τό χερούλι]
hand luggage to sak-v*oo*a-yaz [τό
  σάκ-βουαγιάζ]
handmade kheerop*ee*-eeto [χειροποίητο]
handsome *o*reos [ώραῖος]
hanger m*ee*a krem*a*stra [μιά κρεμάστρα]
hangover: I've got a terrible hangover
  est*h*an*o*me apess*ee*a met*a* to kht*h*ess*ee*no
  met*h*ess*ee* [αἰσθάνομαι ἀπαίσια μετά τό
  χθεσινό μεθύσι]
  my head is killing me to kef*a*lee moo me
  pet*h*enee [τό κεφάλι μου μέ πεθαίνει]
happen: I don't know how it happened the
  ksero pos seen*e*vee [δέν ξέρω πῶς συνέβει]
  what's happening/happened? tee
  seemv*e*nee/seen*e*vee? [τί συμβαίνει/συνέβει;]
happy efteekheesm*e*nos [εὐτυχισμένος]
harbour to leem*a*nee [τό λιμάνι]
hard skleer*o*s [σκληρός]
  (difficult) th*ee*skolo [δύσκολο]
  hard-boiled egg sf*ee*kto avgo [σφικτό αὐγό]
  push hard spr*o*xe theen*a*ta [σπρῶξε δυνατά]
harm *(noun)* to kako [τό κακό]
hat to kapel*o* [τό καπέλο]
hate: I hate . . . meess*o* . . . [μισῶ . . .]
have *e*kho [ἔχω]
  I have a pain *e*kho ena pon*o* [ἔχω ἕνα πόνο]
  I have no . . . then *e*kho . . . [δέν ἔχω . . .]
  do you have any cigars/a map? *e*khete
  p*oo*ra/ena khart*ee*? [ἔχετε ποῦρα/ἕνα χάρτη;]
  can I have some water/some more? boro na

ekho leego nero/akomee leego? [μπορῶ νά ἔχω
λίγο νερό/ἀκόμη λίγο;]
I have to leave tomorrow prepee na feego
avreeo [πρέπει νά φύγω αὔριο]

hayfever alergeekos peeretos [ἀλλεργικός
πυρετός]

he aftos [αὐτός]
he is ... eene ... [εἶναι ...]
he is staying at Hotel ... menee sto
ksenothokheeo ... [μένει στό ξενοδοχεῖο ...]

head to kefalee [τό κεφάλι]
headache ponokefalos [πονοκέφαλος]
headlight faros [φάρος]
head waiter arkheeserveetoros
[ἀρχησερβιτόρος]
head wind enanteeos anemos
[ἐνάντιος ἄνεμος]

health eegeea [ὑγεία]
your health! steen ee-ya soo [στήν ὑγειά σου]

healthy ee-yee-ees [ὑγιής]

hear: I can't hear then boro nakoosso [δέν
μπορῶ ν' ἀκούσω]
hearing aid akoosteeka [ἀκουστικά]

heart ee kartheea [ἡ καρδιά]
heart attack kartheeakee prosvolee
[καρδιακή προσβολή]

heat zestasseea [ζεστασιά]
heat stroke eeleeassee [ἡλίαση]

heating ee thermanssee [ἡ θέρμανση]

heavy varees [βαρύς]

heel to takoonee [τό τακούνι]
could you put new heels on these? boreete
na moo valete kenoorgeea takooneea safta?
[μπορεῖτε νά βάλετε καινούργια τακούνια σ'
αὐτά;]

height to eepsos [τό ὕψος]

hello ya soo [γεία σου]

help (noun) voeetheea [βοήθεια]
can you help me? boreete na me
voeetheessete? [μπορεῖτε νά μέ βοηθείσετε;]

help! vo*eeth*eea! [βοήθεια!]
her af*tee* [αὐτή]
  I like her moo ar*e*ssee [μοῦ ἀρέσει]
  with her ma*z*ee tees [μαζύ της]
  it's her bag, it's hers *ee*ne ee tss*a*nda tees,
  *ee*ne th*ee*k*ee*a tees [εἶναι ἡ τσάντα της, εἶναι
  δικιά της]
  that's hers *ee*ne theek*o* tees [εἶναι δικό της]
here eth*o* [ἐδῶ]
  come here *e*la eth*o* [ἔλα ἐδῶ]
high ps*ee*la [ψηλά]
hill o l*o*fos [ὁ λόφος]
  up/down the hill o an*ee*foros/o kat*ee*foros
  [ὁ ἀνήφορος/ὁ κατήφορος]
him af*ton* [αὐτόν]
  I don't know him then ton ks*e*ro [δέν τόν
  ξέρω]
  with him ma*z*ee too [μαζύ του]
hire *see* **rent**
his: it's his drink, it's his *ee*ne to pot*o* too, *ee*ne
  theek*o* too [εἶναι τό ποτό του, εἶναι δικό του]
hit: he hit me me kt*ee*peesse [μέ κτύπησε]
hitch-hike oto-stop [ὄτο-στόπ]
  hitch-hiker k*a*nee oto-stop [κάνει ὄτο-στόπ]
hold *(verb)* krat*o* [κρατῶ]
hole ee tr*ee*pa [ἡ τρύπα]
holiday th*ee*akopes [διακοπές]
  I'm on holiday *ee*me se th*ee*akopes [εἶμαι σέ
  διακοπές] *see* **public**
home to sp*ee*tee [τό σπίτι]
  I want to go home th*e*lo na pa*o* sp*ee*tee [θέλω
  νά πάω σπίτι]
  at home sto sp*ee*tee [στό σπίτι]
  homesick nostalg*o* to sp*ee*tee moo [νοσταλγῶ
  τό σπίτι μου]
honest t*ee*meeos [τίμιος]
  honestly? log*o* teem*ee*s? [λόγω τιμῆς;]
honey to m*e*lee [τό μέλι]
  honeymoon o m*ee*nas too m*e*leetos [ὁ μήνας
  τοῦ μέλιτος]

hope ee elp*ee*tha [ή έλπίδα]
  I hope that... elp*ee*zo o*tee*... [έλπίζω ότι]
  I hope so/not elp*ee*zo ne/okhee [έλπίζω ναί/όχι]
horn *(car)* to kl*a*xon [τό κλάξον]
horrible freektos [φρικτός]
hors d'oeuvre orekt*ee*ka [όρεκτικά]
horse to *a*logo [τό άλογο]
hospital to nosokom*ee*o [τό νοσοκομεῖο]
  » *TRAVEL TIP: see* **doctor**
host o eekothesspot*ee*s [ό οίκοδεσπότης]
hostess ee eekoth*e*ssp*ee*na [ή οίκοδέσποινα]
  (air) ee aeross*ee*nothos [ή άεροσυνοδός]
hot zesto [ζεστό]
  (spiced) peek*a*nd*ee*ko [πικάντικο]
hotel to ksenothokh*ee*o [τό ξενοδοχεῖο]
hour ee ora [ή ὥρα]
house to sp*ee*tee [τό σπίτι]
  housewife ee eekok*ee*ra [ή οίκοκυρά]
how pos [πῶς]
  how many poss*ee* [πόσοι]
  how much poss*a* [πόσα]
  how often k*a*the pote [κάθε πότε]
  how long posso kero [πόσο καιρό]
  how long have you been here? posso kero eesst*e* etho? [πόσο καιρο εῖστε ἐδῶ;]
  how are you? tee kan*ee*s? [τί κάνεις;]
hull to skar*ee* [τό σκαρί]
humid eegros [ὑγρός]
humour h*u*mor [χιούμορ]
  haven't you got a sense of humour? then ekh*ee*s k*a*tholoo h*u*mor? [δέν ἔχεις καθόλου χιούμορ;]
hundredweight:
  » *TRAVEL TIP: 1 cwt =50.8 kilos*
hungry: I'm hungry/not hungry peen*a*o/then peen*a*o [πεινάω/δέν πεινάω]
hurry: I'm in a hurry vee*a*zome [βιάζομαι]
  please hurry! pe*e*o gr*e*egora parakal*o*! [πιό γρήγορα παρακαλῶ]

hurt: it hurts pon*a*ee [πονάει]
   my leg hurts pon*a*ee to pothee moo [πονάει τό
   πόδι μου]
   YOU MAY THEN HEAR...
   *ee*ne theenat*o*s ponos? *is it a sharp pain?*
husband: my husband o sseezeeg*o*s moo
   [ό σύζυγός μου]
I eg*o* [ἐγώ]
   I am English/a teacher *ee*me
   A*n*glos/th*a*sskalos [εἶμαι ᾿Αγγλος/δάσκαλος]
   I am hot/I'm staying here zesten*o*me/m*e*no
   eth*o* [ζεσταίνομαι/μένω ἐδώ]
ice o p*a*gos [ό πάγος]
   ice-cream ena pagot*o* [ἕνα παγωτό]
   iced coffee kaf*e* frap*e* [καφέ φραπέ]
   with lots of ice me pol*ee* pago [μέ πολύ πάγο]
identity papers ee taft*o*tees [ἡ ταυτότης]
idiot o vl*a*kas [ό βλάκας]
if an [ἄν]
ignition ee m*ee*za [ἡ μίζα]
ill *a*rostos [ἄρρωστος]
   I feel ill *ee*me *a*rostos [εἶμαι ἄρρωστος]
illegal paranomos [παράνομος]
illegible theessana*g*nosto [δυσανάγνωστο]
illness ee aross*t*eea [ἡ ἀρρώστεια]
immediately am*e*ssos [ἀμέσως]
import *(noun)* eess*a*go [εἰσάγω]
important spooth*e*os [σπουδαῖος]
   it's very important *ee*ne pol*ee* seemandeek*o*
   [εἶναι πολύ σημαντικό]
import duty o f*o*ros eessagog*ee*s [ό φόρος
   εἰσαγωγῆς]
impossible ath*ee*naton [ἀδύνατον]
impressive endeeposs*ee*ako [ἐντυπωσιακό]
improve velt*ee*ono [βελτιώνω]
   I want to improve my... *the*lo na
   velt*ee*osso... [θέλω νά βελτιώσω...]
in sto [στό]
inch m*ee*a *ee*ntssa [μία ἴντσα]
  » *TRAVEL TIP: 1 inch = 254 cm*

include pereelamvano [περιλαμβάνω]
  does that include breakfast? aft*o*
  pereelamvan*ee* ke to proeen*o*? [αὐτό
  περιλαμβάνει καί τό πρωϊνό;]
inclusive seemberee-lamvanom*e*noo
  [συμπεριλαμβανομένου]
incompetent an*ee*konos [ἀνίκανος]
inconsiderate aper*ee*skeptos [ἀπερίσκεπτος]
incontinent *a*ssotos [ἄσωτος]
incredible ekpleekteekos [ἐκπληκτικός]
indecent aprep*ee*s [ἀπρεπής]
independent anex*a*rteetos [ἀνεξάρτητος]
India Inth*ee*a ['Ινδία]
Indian Inth*o*s ['Ινδός]
indicator th*ee*ktees por*ee*as [δείκτης πορείας]
indigestion theesspeps*ee*a [δυσπεψία]
indoors sto sp*ee*tee [στό σπίτι]
industry ee veeomeekhan*ee*a [ἡ βιομηχανία]
infection ee m*o*leensee [ἡ μόλυνση]
infectious koleeteekos [κολλητικός]
inflation o plee*th*oreesm*o*s [ὁ πληθωρισμός]
informal anep*ee*sseemos [ἀνεπίσημος]
information pleerofor*ee*-es
  [πληροφορίες]
  **do you have any information in English
  about . . .?** m*ee*pos *e*khete pleerofor*ee*-es sta
  angleek*a* ya . . .? [μήπως ἔχετε πληροφορίες στά
  'Αγγλικά γιά . . .;]
  is there an information office? eep*a*rkhee
  grafe*eo* pleerofore*e*on? [ὑπάρχει γραφεῖο
  πληροφοριῶν;]
inhabitant o k*a*teekos [ὁ κάτοικος]
injection me*e*a *e*nessee [μιά ἔνεση]
injured travmateesm*e*nos [τραυματισμένος]
  he's been injured travmat*ee*steeke
  [τραυματίστηκε]
injury to tr*a*vma [τό τραῦμα]
innocent at*h*o-os [ἄθῶος]
insect *e*na zo*ee*feeo [ἕνα ζωΰφιο]
  insect repellent endomokt*o*no [ἐντομοκτόνο]

inside messa [μέσα]

insist: I insist (on it) epeemeno [ἐπιμένω]

insomnia a-eepneea [ἀϋπνία]

instant coffee nescafe

instead, instead of andee [ἀντί]

can I have that one instead? boro na ekho ekeeno andee aftoo? [μπορῶ νά ἔχω ἐκεῖνο ἀντί αὐτοῦ;]

insulating tape monoteekee teneea [μονωτική ταινία]

insulation ee monossee [ἡ μόνωση]

insult ee prosvolee [ἡ προσβολή]

insurance ee assfaleea [ἡ ἀσφάλεια]

intelligent ekseepnos [ἔξυπνος]

interesting entheeaferon [ἐνδιαφέρον]

international thee-ethnees [διεθνής]

interpreter thee-ermeeneas [διερμηνέας]

would you interpret for us? boreete na metafrassete ya mas? [μπορεῖτε να μεταφράσετε γιά μᾶς;]

into messa [μέσα]

introduce: can I introduce . . .? boro na sas seessteesso . . .? [μπορῶ νά σᾶς συστήσω . . .;]

invalid *(noun)* o anapeeros [ὁ ἀνάπηρος]

invalid chair anapeereekee karekla [ἀναπηρική καρέκλα]

invitation proskleessee [πρόσκληση]

thank you for the invitation efkhareesto ya teen proskleessee [εὐχαριστῶ γιά τήν πρόσκληση]

invite: can I invite you out? borona sas proskalesso na vgoome exo? [μπορῶ νά σᾶς προσκαλέσω νά βγοῦμε ἔξω;]

Ireland Irlantheea ['Ιρλανδία]

Irish Irlanthos ['Ιρλανδος]

iron *(for clothes) (noun)* ena eelektreeko seethero [ἕνα ἠλεκτρικό σίδερο]

will you iron these for me? boreete na moo seetherossete afta? [μπορεῖτε νά μοῦ σιδερώσετε αὐτά;]

ironmonger's to pseeleekadzeetheeko [τό ψιλικατζίδικο]

» *TRAVEL TIP: typically a general store in Greece (not for food though); will sell books and stamps*

is eene [εἶναι]

island to neessee [τό νησί]

it afto [αὐτό]

 it is . . . eene . . . [εἶναι . . .]

Italian Italos ['Ιταλός]

Italy Italeea ['Ιταλία]

itch fagoora [φαγούρα]

 it itches me troee [μέ τρώει]

itemize: would you itemize it for me? boreete na moo to katagrapsete? [μπορεῖτε νά μοῦ τό καταγράψετε;]

jack o greelos [ὁ γρύλος]

jacket to sakakee [τό σακάκι]

jam to gleeko [τό γλυκό]

 traffic jam boteeleeareesma [μποτιλιάρισμα]

January Eeanoo-areeos ['Ιανουάριος]

jaw to sagonee [τό σαγόνι]

jealous zeeleearees [ζηλιάρης]

jeans jeans [τζήνς]

jellyfish meea tsookhtra [μιά τσούχτρα]

jetty o molos [ὁ μῶλος]

jewellery ta kosmeemata [τά κοσμήματα]

jib flokos [φλόκος]

job ee thooleea [ἡ δουλειά]

 just the job afto akreevos [αὐτό ἀκριβῶς]

joke *(noun)* asteeo [ἀστεῖο]

 you must be joking astee-evesse seegoora [ἀστειεύεσαι σίγουρα]

journey to taxeethee [τό ταξίδι]

 have a good journey kalo taxeethee [καλό ταξίδι]

July Ee-ooleeos ['Ιούλιος]

jumper to poolover [τό πουλόβερ]

junction ee theea-stavrossee [ἡ διασταύρωση]

June Ee-ooneeos ['Ιούνιος]

junk koorelaree-es [κουρελαρίες]

just: just two mono theeo [μόνο δύο]
  just there ekee akreevos [ἐκεῖ ἀκριβῶς]
  not just now okhee tora amessos [ὄχι τώρα ἀμέσως]
  just now molees tora [μόλις τώρα]; *(a little while ago)* preen apo leego [πρίν ἀπό λίγο]
  that's just right afto eena otee prepee [αὐτό εἶναι ὅτι πρέπει]

keen: I'm very keen to . . . thelo polee na . . . [θέλω πολύ νά . . .]
  I'm not keen then poleethelo [δέν πολυθέλω]

keep: can I keep it? boro na to krateesso [μπορῶ νά τό κρατήσω]
  you keep it parto essee [πάρ' το ἐσύ]
  keep the change krata ta ressta [κράτα τά ρέστα]
  you didn't keep your promise then krateesses teen eepo-skhessee soo [δέν κράτησες τήν ὑπόσχεσή σου]

kettle o vrasteeras [ὁ βραστήρας]
key to kleethee [τό κλειδί]
kidney to nefro [τό νεφρό]
kill *(verb)* skotono [σκοτώνω]
kilo to kilo [τό κιλό]

» *TRAVEL TIP: conversion:* $\dfrac{kilos}{5} \times 11 = pounds$

kilos	1	1½	5	6	7	8	9
pounds	2.2	3.3	11	13.2	15.4	17.6	19.8

kilometre kheeleeometro [χιλιόμετρο]

» *TRAVEL TIP: conversion:* $\dfrac{kilometres}{8} \times 5 = miles$

kilometres	1	5	10	20	50	100
miles	0.62	3.11	6.2	12.4	31	62

kind: that's very kind of you afto eene polee evgeneeko ek meroos sas [αὐτό εἶναι πολύ εὐγενικό ἐκ μέρους σας]

kiosk to pereeptero [τό περίπτερο]
» *TRAVEL TIP: at kiosks on the street you can buy tobacco, books, chocolate, soft drinks etc; they also have telephones and sell stamps*

kiss *(noun)* ena feel*ee* [ἕνα φιλί]
kitchen ee koo*zee*na [ἡ κουζίνα]
knee to gonato [τό γόνατο]
knickers ee kee*l*ota [ἡ κυλόττα]
knife ena mak*heree* [ἕνα μαχαίρι]
knock *(verb)* k*t*eepo [κτυπῶ]
   there's a knocking noise from the engine
   ak*oo*gete enas metalee*k*os *th*oreevos apo *tee*
   meekhan*ee* [ἀκούγετε ἕνας μεταλικός θόρυβος
   ἀπό τή μηχανή]
know ksero [ξέρω]
   I don't know then ksero [δέν ξέρω]
label *(noun)* ee eteeketa [ἡ ἐτικέττα]
laces *(shoe)* kortho*neea* [κορδόνια]
lacquer ee lak [ἡ λάκ]
ladies *(toilet)* geenekon [γυναικῶν]
lady meea keer*eea* [μιά κυρία]
lager beera [μπύρα]
   lager and lime beera me 'lime' [μπύρα μέ λάϊμ]
lamb *(meat)* arnee [ἀρνί]
lamp ee lampa [ἡ λάμπα]
   lampshade ena amba*z*oor [ἕνα ἀμπαζούρ]
   lamp-post o steelos [ὁ στῦλος]
land *(noun)* ee yee [ἡ γῆ]
lane *(car)* ee loreetha [ἡ λωρίδα]
language glossa [γλώσσα]
large megalos [μεγάλος]
laryngitis lareengeetees [λαρυγγίτης]
last telefteos [τελευταῖος]
   last year/week ton perasmeno khrono/teen
   perasmenee evthomatha [τόν περασμένο
   χρόνο/τήν περασμένη ἑβδομάδα]
   last night kh-*th*ess vrathee [χθές βράδυ]
   at last! epee teloos! [ἐπί τέλους!]
late: sorry I'm late me seen-khor*ee*te poo
   *a*rgeessa [μέ συγχωρήτε που ἄργησα]
   it's a bit late *ee*ne kapos arga [εἶναι κάπως
   *a*rgá]
   please hurry, I'm late pe*eo* greegora
   parakal*o*, *e*kho arg*ee*ssee [πιό γρήγορα

παρακαλῶ, ἔχω ἀργήσει]
at the latest to argotero [τό ἀργότερο]
later argotera [ἀργότερα]
see you later *th*a se tho argotera [θά σέ δῶ
ἀργότερα]
latitude to geografeeko pl*a*tos [τό γεωγραφικό
πλάτος]
laugh (*verb*) ye-lo [γελῶ]
launderette to pleend*ee*reeo [τό πλυντήριο]
lavatory ee tooal*e*ta [ἡ τουαλέττα]
law o n*o*mos [ὁ νόμος]
lawyer theek*ee*goros [δικηγόρος]
laxative kath*a*rseeo [καθάρσιο]
lay-by to parking [τό πάρκινγκ]
lazy temb*e*lees [τεμπέλης]
leaf to f*ee*lo [τό φύλλο]
leak (*noun*) ee theear*oe*e [ἡ διαρροή]
it leaks st*a*zee [στάζει]
learn: I want to learn . . . *the*lo na m*a*tho . . .
[θέλω νά μάθω . . .]
lease (*verb*) neek*ee*azo [νοικιάζω]
least: not in the least k*a*thol*oo* [καθόλου]
at least tool*a*kheesston [τουλάχιστον]
leather th*e*rma [δέρμα]
this meat's like leather af*to* to kre*a*seene san
s*o*la [αὐτό τό κρέας εἶναι σάν σόλα]
leave: we're leaving tomorrow f*e*vgome
avr*ee*o [φεύγομε αὔριο]
when does the bus leave? pote f*e*vgee to
leofor*ee*o? [πότε φεύγει τό λεωφορεῖο;]
I left two shirts in my room af*ee*ssa th*ee*o
poka*mee*ssa sto thom*a*teeo moo [ἄφησα δύο
πουκάμισα στό δωμάτιο μου]
can I leave this here? boro naf*ee*sso af*to* eth*o*?
[μπορῶ ν' ἀφήσω αὐτό ἐδῶ;]
left areest*e*ra [ἀριστερά]
on the left pros tareest*e*ra [πρός τ' ἀριστερά]
left-handed areest*e*ros [ἀριστερός]

» *TRAVEL TIP: the word for 'left-handed' in Greek*
also means 'communist'

left luggage (office) khoros felaxeos aposkevon [χώρος φυλάξεως ἀποσκευῶν]

leg to pothee [τό πόδι]

legal nomeemos [νόμιμος]

lemon ena lemonee [ἕνα λεμόνι]

lemonade meea lemonatha [μιά λεμονάδα]

lend: will you lend me your . . .? borees na moo thaneessees . . .? [μπορεῖς νά μοῦ δανείσεις . . .;]

lengthen makreno [μακραίνω]

lens o fakos [ὁ φακός]

Lent ee sarakostee [ἡ Σαρακοστή]

less leegoteros [λιγότερος]

    less than that leegotero apo ekeeno [λιγότερο ἀπ᾽ ἐκεῖνο]

let: let me help asse me na voeetheeso [ἄσε με νά βοηθήσω]

    let me go! asse me na feego! [ἄσε με νά φύγω!]

    will you let me off here? borees na me afeessees na katevo etho? [μπορεῖς νά μέ ἀφήσεις νά κατέβω ἐδῶ;]

    let's go pame [πᾶμε]

letter to grama [τό γράμμα]

    are there any letters for me? ekho kanena grama? [ἔχω κανένα γράμμα;]

    letterbox takheethromeeko kootee [ταχυδρομικό κουτί]

lettuce to maroolee [τό μαρούλι]

level-crossing eessopethe theeavassee [ἰσόπεδη διάβαση]

liable *(responsible)* eepeftheenos [ὑπεύθυνος]

library ee veevleeotheekee [ἡ βιβλιοθήκη]

licence ee atheea [ἡ ἄδεια]

lid to kapakee [τό καπάκι]

lie *(noun)* ena psema [ἕνα ψέμα]

    can he lie down for a bit? boree na ksaplossee ya leego? [μπορεῖ νά ξαπλώσει γιά λίγο;]

life ee zoee [ἡ ζωή]

    life assurance asfaleea zoees [ἀσφάλεια ζωῆς]

    lifebelt, life jacket to sosseeveeo [τό σωσίβιο]

lifeboat ee sos*ee*veeos le*m*vos [ἡ σωσίβιος λέμβος]
life-guard o navagos*so*stees [ὁ ναυαγοσώστης]
lift: do you want a lift? *the*lete na sas p*a*o? [θέλετε νά σᾶς πάω;]
could you give me a lift? bor*ee*te na me p*a*te? [μπορεῖτε νά μέ πάτε;]
the lift isn't working o anelkees*tee*ras then thoole*ve*e [ὁ ἀνελκυστήρας δέν δουλεύει]
light: the lights aren't working ta f*o*ta then an*a*voon [τά φῶτα δέν ἀνάβουν]
have you got a light? e*khe*te fote*a*a? [ἔχετε φωτιά;]
when it gets light *o*tan kseemer*o*ssee [ὅταν ξημερώσει]
light bulb la*m*pa [λάμπα]
light meter foto*me*tro [φωτόμετρο]
(not heavy) elaf*ros* [ἐλαφρός]
like: would you like ...? t*ha the*late ...? [θά θέλατε ...;]
I'd like a .../I'd like to ... t*ha ee*th*e*la ena .../th*a ee*th*e*la na ... [θά εἴθελα ἕνα .../θά εἴθελα νά ...]
I like it/you moo ar*e*ssee/moo ar*e*ssees [μοῦ ἀρέσει/μοῦ ἀρέσεις]
I don't like it then moo ar*e*ssee [δέν μοῦ ἀρέσει]
what's it like? me tee mee*a*zee? [μέ τί μοιάζει;]
do it like this k*a*ne to e*t*ssee [κάνε το ἔτσι]
lime 'lime' [λάϊμ]
line gram*ee* [γραμμή]
lip to k*hee*lee [τό χείλι]
lip salve voo*tee*ro kak*a*o [βούτυρο κακάο]
lipstick kokeen*a*thee [κοκκινάδι]
liqueur ena lee*ker* [ἕνα λικέρ]
list *(noun)* o kat*a*logos [ὁ κατάλογος]
listen ak*oo*-o [ἀκούω]
litre ena lee*tro* [ἕνα λίτρο]
» *TRAVEL TIP: 1 litre = 1½ pints = 0.22 gals*

little meekros [μικρός]
  a little ice/a little more leego pago/akomee leego [λίγο πάγο/ἀκόμη λίγο]
  just a little mono leego [μόνο λίγο]
live zo [ζῶ] **I live in Glasgow** meno stee Glasskovee [μένω στή Γλασκώβη]
  where do you live? poo menees? [ποῦ μένεις;]
liver to seekotee [τό συκώτι]
lizard ee savra [ἡ σαύρα]
loaf meea frandzola [μιά φραντζόλα]
lobster o astakos [ὁ ἀστακός]
local: could we try a local wine? boroome na thokeemassome to dopeeo krassee? [μποροῦμε νά δοκιμάσομε τό ντόπιο κρασί;]
  a local restaurant ena esteeatoreeo tees pereeokhees [ἕνα ἐστιατόριο τῆς περιοχῆς]
lock: the lock's broken ee kleethareea eene spasmenee [ἡ κλειδαριά εἶναι σπασμένη]
  I've locked myself out kleethotheeka exo [κλειδώθηκα ἔξω]
lonely monakheekos [μοναχικός]
long makrees [μακρής]
  we'd like to stay longer tha thelame na mename pereessotero [θά θέλαμε νά μέναμε περισσότερο]
  that was long ago afto eetane preen apo polee kero [αὐτό ἤτανε πρίν ἀπό πολύ καιρό]
longitude geografeeko meekos [γεωγραφικό μῆκος]
loo: where's the loo? pooeene ee tooaleta? [ποῦ εἶναι ἡ τουαλέττα;]
look: you look tired fenesse koorasmenos [φαίνεσαι κουρασμένος]
  I'm looking forward to . . . pereemeno me aneepomoneesseea na . . . [περιμένω μέ ἀνυπομονησία νά . . .]
  I'm looking for . . . psakhno ya . . . [ψάχνω γιά . . .]
  look out! prossekhe! [πρόσεχε!]
loose khalaros [χαλαρός]

lorry to forteego [τό φορτηγό]
  lorry driver otheegos forteegoo [ὁδηγός
  φορτηγοῦ]
lose khano [χάνω]
  I've lost my bag ekhassa teen tsanta moo
  [ἔχασα τήν τσάντα μου]
  excuse me, I'm lost me seen-khoreete, ekho
  khathee [μέ συγχωρεῖτε, ἔχω χαθεῖ]
lost property apolesthenda [ἀπολεσθέντα]
lot: a lot/not a lot pola/okhee pola [πολλά/ὄχι
  πολλά]
  a lot of chips/wine poles patates
  teeganeetes/polee krassee [πολλές πατάτες
  τηγανιτές/πολύ κρασί]
  a lot more expensive polee peeo akreevo
  [πολύ πιό ἀκριβό]
  lots pola [πολλά]
lotion ee losseeon [ἡ λοσιόν]
loud theenata [δυνατά]
  louder peeo theenata [πιό δυνατά]
love: I love you sagapo [σ' ἀγαπῶ]
  do you love me? magapas? [μ' ἀγαπᾶς;]
  he's in love eene erotevmenos [εἶναι
  ἐρωτευμένος]
  I love this wine maressee afto to krassee
  [μ' ἀρέσει αὐτό τό κρασί]
lovely oreos [ὡραῖος]
low khameelos [χαμηλός]
luck ee teekhee [ἡ τύχη]
  good luck! kalee teekhee! [καλή τύχη!]
lucky teekheros [τυχερός]
  you're lucky eesse teekheros [εἶσαι τυχερός]
  that's lucky afto eene teekhero
  [αὐτό εἶναι τυχερό]
luggage ee aposkeves [οἱ ἀποσκεύες]
lumbago to loombako [τό λουμπάκο]
lump to preexeemo [τό πρήξιμο]
lunch to ye-vma [τό γεῦμα]
lung o pnevmonas [ὁ πνεύμωνας]
luxurious poleetelees [πολυτελής]

luxury poleetel*ee*as [πολυτελείας]
mad tre*l*os [τρελλός]
madam keer*ee*a [κυρία]
made-to-measure ram*e*no ka*t*a parangel*ee*a
  [ραμένο κατά παραγγελία]
magazine to pereeo*th*eeko [τό περιοδικό]
magnificent magaloprep*ee*s [μεγαλοπρεπής]
maiden name patron*ee*mo [πατρώνυμο]
mail gra*m*ata [γράμματα]
mainland sto essoter*ee*ko tees khoras [στό
  ἐσωτερικό τῆς χώρας]
main road o kendr*ee*kos *th*romos [ὁ κεντρικός
  δρόμος]
make ka*n*o [κάνω]
  will we make it in time? *th*a prolavome? [θά
  προλάβομε;]
  make-up to make-up [τό μέϊκ ἄπ]
man o *a*n*th*ras [ὁ ἄνδρας]
manager o *th*ee*a*kheer*ee*es*t*ees [ὁ διαχειρηστής]
  can I see the manager? boro na *th*o ton
  dee*a*kheer*ee*es*t*ee? [μπορῶ νά δῶ τόν
  διαχειρηστή;]
manicure maneekee*oo*r [μανικιούρ]
manners ee tropee [οἱ τρόποι]
many pol*ee* [πολλοί]
map o khar*t*ees [ὁ χάρτης]
  a map of Athens ena khar*t*ee tees A*th*ee*n*as
  [ἕνα χάρτη τῆς Ἀθήνας]
March Mar*t*eeos [Μάρτιος]
margarine ee margar*ee*nee [ἡ μαργαρίνη]
marina ee provl*ee*ta [ἡ προβλήτα]
mark: there's a mark on it ekhee ena
  seema*th*ee [ἔχει ἕνα σημάδι]
market, marketplace ee agora [ἡ ἀγορά]
marmalade ee marmela*th*a [ἡ μαρμελάδα]
married pandre*m*enos [πανδρεμένος]
marry: will you marry me? *th*a me
  pandref*t*ees? [θά μέ πανδρευτεῖς;]
marvellous *th*avmasseeos [θαυμάσιος]
mascara ee maskara [ἡ μασκάρα]

....

mashed potatoes pata*tes* poor*e* [πατάτες πουρέ]
massage 'massage' [μασάζ]
mast to katar*tee* [τό κατάρτι]
mat khal*akee* [χαλάκι]
match *e*na sp*ee*rto [ἕνα σπίρτο]
  a box of matches *e*na koot*ee* speerta [ἕνα κουτί σπίρτα]
  football match pothossfereek*o*s ag*o*nas [ποδοσφαιρικός ἀγώνας]
material eeleek*o* [ὑλικό]
matter: it doesn't matter then peer*a*zee [δέν πειράζει]
  what's the matter? tee seemben*ee*? [τί συμβαίνει;]
mattress to str*o*ma [τό στρῶμα]
mature *o*reemos [ὥριμος]
maximum m*e*geestos [μέγιστος]
May M*a*eeos [Μάϊος]
may: may I have . . .? *th*a boroossa na*e*kho . . .? [θά μπορούσα νά ἔχω . . .;]
maybe bor*ee* [μπορεῖ]
mayonnaise mageeon*e*za [μαγιονέζα]
me ego [ἐγώ]
  can you hear me? mak*oo*s? [μ' ἀκούς;]
  please give it to me se parakal*o* th*o*sse moo to [σέ παρακαλῶ δῶσε μου τό]
meal ye-vma [γεῦμα]
mean: what does this mean? tee en*o*ee af*to*? [τί ἐννοεῖ αὐτό;]
measles eelar*a* [ἰλαρά]
  German measles ereethr*a* [ἐρυθρά]
measurements m*e*tra [μέτρα]
meat to kr*e*as [τό κρέας]
mechanic: is there a mechanic here? eepar*k*hee kan*e*nas meekhaneek*o*s eth*o*? [ὑπάρχει κανένας μηχανικός ἐδῶ;]
medicine to far*m*ako [τό φάρμακο]
meet seenand*o* [συναντῶ]
  pleased to meet you kher*o*me poo sas gnor*ee*zo [χαίρομαι πού σᾶς γνωρίζω]

when can we meet again? pote boro na se ksanatho? [πότε μπορῶ νά σέ ξαναδῶ;]

meeting seenandeesee [συνάντηση]

melon peponee [πεπόνι]

member melos [μέλος]

how do I become a member? pos boro na geeno melos? [πῶς μπορῶ νά γίνω μέλος;]

men ee anthres [οἱ ἄνδρες]

mend: can you mend this? boreete na epeeskevassete afto? [μπορεῖτε νά ἐπισκευάσετε αὐτό;]

mention: don't mention it parakalo [παρακαλῶ]

menu katalogos fageeton [κατάλογος φαγητῶν]

can I have the menu, please? boro na ekho ton katalogo, parakalo? [μπορῶ νά ἔχω τόν κατάλογο, παρακαλῶ;] see pages 69–71

mess anakatoma [ἀνακάτωμα]

message: are there any messages for me? eeparkhee kanena meeneema ya mena? [ὑπάρχει κανένα μήνυμα γιά μένα;]

can I leave a message for . . .? boro nafeesso ena meeneema ya . . .? [μπορῶ ν' ἀφήσω ἕνα μήνυμα γιά . . .;]

metre to metro [τό μέτρο]

» TRAVEL TIP: 1 metre = 39.37 ins = 1.09 yds

midday messeemeree [μεσημέρι]

middle messo [μέσο]

in the middle stee messee [στή μέση]

midnight messaneekta [μεσάνυκτα]

might: I might be late boree nargeesso [μπορεῖ ν' ἀργήσω]; **he might have gone** boree nakhee feegee [μπορεῖ νἄχει φύγει]

migraine eemeekraneea [ἡμικρανία]

mild eepeeos [ἤπιος]

mile ena meelee [ἕνα μίλι]

» TRAVEL TIP: conversion: $\frac{miles}{5} \times 8$ = kilometres

miles	$\frac{1}{2}$	1	3	5	10	50	100
kilometres	0.8	1.6	4.8	8	16	80	160

ΟΡΕΚΤΙΚΑ   ΟRΕΚΤΕΕΚΑ   APPETISERS

Ντολμαδάκια   Dolmadakia
vine leaves stuffed with minced meat, rice and
herbs

Μελιτζανοσαλάτα   Melitzanosalata
eggplant salad

Κεφτέδες   Keftedes
meat balls

Ταραμοσαλάτα   Taramosalata
fish roe pâté

Σπανακόπιτα   Spanakopita
spinach squares

Χταπόδι   Khtapothee
boiled octopus

Σαγανάκι   Saganaki
fried cheese and egg

Σαλάτα χωριάτικη   Salata khoreeateekee
mixed salad

Κολοκυθάκια τηγανιτά   Kolokeethakeea
teeganeeta
fried baby marrows

Κοκορέτσι   Kokoretsi
spit-roasted liver and innards

Τζατζήκι   Tzantziki
a mixture of cucumber, yogurt and garlic –
sounds awful but worth a try!

ΣΟΥΠΕΣ   SOOPES   SOUPS

Αὐγολέμονο   Avgolemono
chicken broth, lemon and egg

Κακαβιά   Kakavia
various kinds of fish

Πατσάς   Patzas
intestines of lamb thoroughly washed and
cut up

Φασολάδα   Fassolatha
hot bean soup

Μαγειρήτσα   Magiritsa
traditional lamb soup served on the Saturday
night before Easter Sunday

Ψαρόσουπα Pssarossoopa
fish soup

MAIN DISHES

Στιφάδο Stifado
hare or rabbit stew with onions
Μουσακᾶ Moussaka
layers of either eggplant or potatoes, minced
meat topped with thick creamy sauce and baked
Γιουβαρλάκια Yiouvarlakia
minced meat, rice and seasoning in sauce
Παστίτσιο Pastichio
macaroni, minced meat and thick creamy sauce
Γιουβέτσι Yiouvetsi
roast lamb with pasta
'Αρνί φρικασέ Arni frikasse
lamb, lettuce and thick white sauce
'Αγκινάρες Agginares
artichokes in light sauce
Τομάτες γεμιστές Domates yemeestes
tomatoes with a stuffing of mince, rice and herbs
Πιπεριές γεμιστές Peeperee-ea yemeestes
stuffed green peppers
Γαριδοπίλαφο Gareethopeelafo
prawns with rice cooked in butter
Λαχανοντολμάδες Lakhanodolmathes
cabbage leaves stuffed with rice and mince

ΘΑΛΑΣΣΙΝΑ THALASSINA   SEAFOOD

Μπακαλιάρος Bakaliaros
cod, fried or boiled
'Αστακός Asstakos
lobster, grilled or boiled
Γαρίδες Gareethes
prawns, grilled or boiled
Καλαμαράκια Kalamarakeea
fried baby squid
Καβούρια Kavoureea
boiled crab

Μύδια   Meetheea
  mussels

ΤΥΡΙΑ	TEEREEA	CHEESES

Μανούρι   Manouri
  hard cheese
Φέτα   Feta
  soft white cheese
Κασέρι   Kasseri
  mild yellow cheese
Κεφαλοτύρι   Kefalotiri
  hard cheese, very salty
'Ανθότυρο   Anthotiro
  aromatic cheese
*Don't expect each cheese to be always consistent in
  taste*

ΓΛΥΚΑ	GLEEKA	SWEETS

Γαλακτομπούρεκο   Galatoboureko
  thin pastry with custard filling
Καταΐφι   Kataifi
  shredded pastry with nuts and honey
Κουραμπιέδες   Kourabiethes
  Greek shortbread
Μελομακάρονα   Melomakarona
  fritters coated in nuts and syrup
'Αμυγδαλοτά   Amigthalota
  almond pastries
Βανίλια   Vanillia
  vanilla-flavoured sweet or ice-cream
Πορτοκάλι   Portokalee
  orange, boiled and sugared
Μπακλαβάς   Baklavas
  pastry filled with nuts and syrup
Βύσσινο   Veesseeno
  cherries, boiled and sugared
Λουκουμάδες   Lookoomathes
  fritters coated in honey
Παγωτό   Pagoto
  ice cream

milk gala [γάλα]
   a glass of milk ena poteeree gala [ένα ποτήρι γάλα]
   milkshake milkshake [μίλκσέϊκ]
millimetre kheelee-osto [χιλιοστό]
milometer to konter [τό κοντέρ]
minced meat o keemas [ό κιμάς]
mind: I've changed my mind alaxa gnomee [άλαξα γνώμη]
   I don't mind then me enokhlee [δέν μέ ἐνοχλεῖ]
   do you mind if I . . .? tha se peeraze an . . .? [θά σέ πείραζε ἄν . . .;]
   never mind then peerazee [δέν πειράζει]
mine theeko moo [δικό μου]
mineral water metaleeko nero [μεταλλικό νερό]
minimum elakheestos [ἐλάχιστος]
minus pleen [πλήν]
minute lepto [λεπτό]
   in a minute se ena lepto [σέ ἕνα λεπτό]
   just a minute ena lepto [ἕνα λεπτό]
mirror o kathreftees [ό καθρέπτης]
Miss thespeenees [Δεσποινής]
miss: I miss you moo leepees [μοῦ λείπεις]
   he's missing leepee [λείπει]
   there is a . . . missing leepee ena . . . [λείπει ἕνα . . .]
mist omeekhlee [ὀμίχλη]
mistake lathos [λάθος]
   I think you've made a mistake nomeezo otee ekhees kanee ena lathos [νομίζω ὅτι ἔχεις κάνει ἕνα λάθος]
misunderstanding parexeegeessee [παρεξήγηση]
modern moderno [μοντέρνο]
Monday Theftera [Δευτέρα]
money lefta [λεφτά]
   I've lost my money ekhassa ta lefta moo [ἔχασα τά λεφτά μου]
month meenas [μῆνας]
moon to fegaree [τό φεγγάρι]

moorings to angeerovoleeo [τό ἀγκυροβόλιο]
moped to meekhanakee [τό μηχανάκι]
more pereessotero [περισσότερο]
    can I have some more? boro na ekho akomee
    leego? [μπορῶ νά ἔχω ἀκόμη λίγο;]
    more wine, please kee alo krassee parakalo
    [κι' ἄλλο κρασί, παρακαλῶ]
    no more ftanee [φτάνει]
    more comfortable peeo anapafteekee [πιό
    ἀναπαυτική]
    more than pereessotero apo [περισσότερο
    ἀπό]
morning proee [πρωΐ]
    good morning kaleemera [καλημέρα]
    in the morning to proee [τό πρωΐ]
    this morning afto to proee [αὐτό τό πρωΐ]
most: I like it the most moo aressee peeo polee
    apo ola [μοῦ ἀρέσει πιό πολύ ἀπό ὅλα]
    most of the time/the people seeneethos/ee
    pereessoteree anthropee [συνήθως/οἱ
    περισσότεροι ἄνθρωποι]
mosquito ena koonoopee [ἕνα κουνούπι]
motel motel [Μοτέλ]
mother: my mother ee meetera moo [ἡ μητέρα
    μου]
motor ee meekhanee [ἡ μηχανή]
motorbike to motossako [τό μοτοσακό]
motorboat varka me meekhanee [βάρκα μέ
    μηχανή]
motorcyclist motosseekleteestees
    [μοτοσυκλετιστής]
motorist otheegos aftokeeneetoo [ὁδηγός
    αὐτοκινήτου]
motorway ethneekee othos [ἐθνική ὁδός]
mountain to voono [τό βουνό]
mouse ena pondeekee [ἕνα ποντίκι]
moustache moostakee [μουστάκι]
mouth to stoma [τό στόμα]
    mouth-watering lee-onee sto stoma [λυώνει
    στό στόμα]

move: don't move mee koonee-*e*sse [μή
κουνιέσαι]

could you move your car? bor*e*ete na
metak*ee*n*ee*ssete to aftok*ee*neeto sas? [μπορείτε
νά μετακινήσετε τό αὐτοκίνητό σας;]

Mr K*ee*reeos [Κος]

Mrs K*ee*ree*a* [Κα]

Ms *no Greek equivalent*

much pol*ee* [πολύ]

much better/much more pol*ee* kal*ee*tera/
per*ee*ssotera [πολύ καλλίτερα/περισσότερα]

not much *o*khee pol*ee* [ὄχι πολύ]

mug: I've been mugged me l*ee*stepsan [μέ
λήστεψαν]

mum mamm*a* [μαμμά]

muscle o mees [ὁ μῦς]

museum to moos*ee*eo [τό μουσεῖο]

mushroom to maneet*a*ree [τό μανιτάρι]

music moos*ee*k*ee* [μουσική]

must: I must have . . . pr*e*pee na *e*kho . . .
[πρέπει νά ἔχω . . .]

I must not eat . . . then pr*e*pee na fa-o . . . [δέν
πρέπει νά φάω . . .]

you must pr*e*pee [πρέπει]

must I? pr*e*pee? [πρέπει;]

mustard moost*a*rtha [μουστάρδα]

my moo [μοῦ]; **my hotel** to ksenothok*ee*eo moo
[τό ξενοδοχεῖο μου]

nail *(finger)* to n*ee*khee [τό νύχι]
(wood) to karf*ee* [τό καρφί]

nailfile mee*a* l*ee*ma neekhee-on [μιά λίμα
νυχιῶν]

nail polish mano [μανό]

nail clippers o neekhokoptees [ὁ νυχοκόπτης]

nail scissors *e*na psal*ee*thee ya n*ee*khee*a* [ἕνα
ψαλίδι γιά νύχια]

naked geemn*o*s [γυμνός]

name *o*noma [ὄνομα]

my name is . . . me l*e*ne . . . [μέ λένε . . .]

what's your name? pos se l*e*ne? [πῶς σέ λένε;]

napkin petsseta [πετσέτα]
nappy pana [πάνα]
narrow steno [στενό]
national ethneekos [ἐθνικός]
nationality ethneekotees [ἐθνικότης]
natural feesseekos [φυσικός]
naughty: don't be naughty meen eesse
  ataktos [μήν εἶσαι ἄτακτος]
near: is it near? eene konda? [εἶναι κοντά;]
  near here etho konda [ἐδῶ κοντά]
  do you go near . . .? pas konda . . .? [πᾶς
  κοντά . . .;]
  where's the nearest . . .? poo eene to
  pleessee-estero . . .? [πού εἶναι τό
  πλησιέστερο . . .;]
nearly skhethon [σχεδόν]
neat *(drink)* sketo [σκέτο]
necessary anangeo [ἀναγκαῖο]
  it's not necessary then khreeazete [δέν
  χρειάζεται]
neck o lemos [ὁ λαιμός]
  necklace to kolee-e [τό κολλιέ]
need: I need a . . . khreeazome ena . . .
  [χρειάζομαι ἕνα . . .]
needle meea velona [μιά βελόνα]
neighbour o yee-tonas [ὁ γείτονας]
neither: neither of them kanenas apo toos
  theeo [κανένας ἀπό τούς δύο]
  neither . . . nor . . . oote . . . oote
  [οὔτε . . . οὔτε]
  neither do I oote kee ego [οὔτε κι' ἐγώ]
nephew: my nephew o anepseeos moo
  [ὁ ἀνεψιός μου]
nervous taragmenos [ταραγμένος]
net *(fishing)* to theektee [τό δίκτυ]
  (hair) o feeles [ὁ φιλές]
  net price katharee teemee [καθαρή τιμή]
never pote [ποτέ]
  well I never! okhee pote! [ὄχι ποτέ!]
new neo [νέο]

New Year Neo etos [Νέο ἔτος]
New Year's Eve Paramonee tees
Protokhroneeas [Παραμονή τῆς Πρωτοχρονιᾶς]
Happy New Year kharoomenee
protokhroneea [Χαρούμενη Πρωτοχρονιά]
» *TRAVEL TIP: the lights are turned out at
midnight; after midnight it's a Greek custom to
play cards*
news ta nea [τά νέα]
　newsagent o efeemereethopolees [ὁ
　ἐφημεριδοπώλης]
　newspaper ee efeemereetha [ἡ ἐφημερίδα]
　do you have any English newspapers?
　ekhete Angleekes efeemereethes?
　[ἔχετε Ἀγγλικές ἐφημερίδες;]
New Zealand Nea Zeelantheea [Νέα Ζηλανδία]
New Zealander Neo Zeelanthos [Νεο Ζηλανδός]
next o epomenos [ὁ ἐπόμενος]
　sit next to me katsse konda moo [κάτσε κοντά
　μου]
　please stop at the next corner parakalo
　stamateeste steen epomenee strofee [παρακαλῶ
　σταματῆστε στήν ἐπόμενη στροφή]
　see you next year tha se tho too khronoo [θά
　σέ δῶ τοῦ χρόνου]
　next week/next Tuesday teen alee
　evthomatha/Treetee [τήν ἄλλη ἐβδομάδα/Τρίτη]
nice kalo [καλό]
niece: my niece ee aneepseea moo [ἡ ἀνηψιά
　μου]
night vrathee [βράδυ]
　good night kaleeneekta [καληνύκτα]
　at night to vrathee [τό βράδυ]
　night porter neektereenos theeroros
　[νυκτερινός θυρωρός]
　is there a good night club here? ekhee
　kanena kalo night club etho? [ἔχει κανένα καλό
　νάϊτ κλάμπ ἐδῶ;]
　night-life neektereenee zoee [νυκτερινή ζωή]
no okhee [ὄχι]

there's no water then ekhee nero [δέν ἔχει νερό]

no way! apoklee-ete [ἀποκλείεται]

I've no money then ekho lefta [δέν ἔχω λεφτά]

» *TRAVEL TIP: rolling the head upwards and back means 'no' in Greece*

nobody kanenas [κανένας]

  nobody saw it kanenas then to eethe [κανένας δέν τό εἶδε]

noisy thoreevothees [θορυβώδης]

  our room is too noisy to thomateeo mas ekhee polee fassareea [τό δωμάτιό μας ἔχει πολύ φασαρία]

none kanees [κανείς]

  none of them kanenas ap aftoos [κανένας ἀπ' αὐτούς]

nonsense anoeessee-es [ἀνοησίες]

normal feesseeologeekos [φυσιολογικός]

north o voras [ὁ βορρᾶς]

Northern Ireland Vorios Irlantheea [Βόρειος Ἰρλανδία]

nose ee meetee [ἡ μύτη]

  nosebleed emorageea apo tee meetee [αἱμοραγία ἀπό τή μύτη]

not then [δέν]

  I'm not hungry then peenao [δέν πεινάω]

  not that one okhee afto [ὄχι αὐτό]

  not me/you okhee ego/essee [ὄχι ἐγώ/ἐσύ]

  not here/there okhee etho/ekee [ὄχι ἐδῶ/ἐκεῖ]

  I do not want to then thelo [δέν θέλω]

  he didn't tell me then moo eepe [δέν μου εἶπε]

note *(bank note)* khartonomeesma [χαρτονόμισμα]

nothing teepote [τίποτε]

November Noemvreeos [Νοέμβριος]

now tora [τώρα]

nowhere poothena [πουθενά]

nudist geemneesstees [γυμνιστής]

  nudist beach paraleea geemneeston [παραλία γυμνιστῶν]

nuisance: it's a nuisance *ee*ne bela*s* [εἶναι μπελᾶς]
    this man's being a nuisance *ee*ne enokhleeteekos [εἶναι ἐνοχλητικός]
numb mootheeasmenos [μουδιασμένος]
number aree*th*mos [ἀριθμός]
    number plate peenake*e*thes [πινακἶδες]
nurse nossokomos [νοσοκόμος]
nut to kareethee [τό καρύδι]
    (for bolt) ena paxeema*t*hee [ἕνα παξιμάδι]
oar to koopee [τό κουπί]
obligatory eepokhreoteeka [ὑποχρεωτικά]
obviously profanos [προφανῶς]
occasionally kameea fora [καμιά φορά]
occupied kateeleemenee [κατειλημμένη]
    is this seat occupied? *ee*ne kateeleemenee af*t*ee ee *t*hessee? [εἶναι κατειλημμένη αὐτή ἡ θέση;]
o'clock *see* **time**
October Oktovreeos [᾿Οκτώβριος]
octopus khtapothee [χταπόδι]
odd *(number)* monos [μονός]
    (strange) paraxenos [παράξενος]
of too [τοῦ]
off: the milk/meat is off to ga*l*a/kreas kha*l*asse [τό γάλα/κρέας χάλασε]
    it just came off molees vgeeke [μόλις βγῆκε]
    10% off theka tees ekato ekptossee [10% ἔκπτωση]
offence prosvolee [προσβολή]
office grafeeo [γραφεῖο]
officer *(to policeman)* keeree-e assteenome [κύριε ἀστυνόμε]
official *(noun)* epeesseemos [ἐπίσημος]
often seekhna [συχνά]
    not often okhee seekhna [ὄχι συχνά]
oil lathee [λάδι]
    will you change the oil? boreete nala*x*ete ta latheea? [μπορεῖτε ν' ἀλλάξετε τά λάδια;]
ointment aleefee [ἀλοιφή]
OK endaxee [ἐντάξει]

old ye-ros [γέρος]
   how old are you? posso khronon eese? [πόσο χρονῶν εἶσαι;]
   I am 25 eeme 25 khronon [εἶμαι 25 χρονῶν]
olive ee eleea [ἡ ἐλιά]
   olive oil eleolatho [ἐλεόλαδο]
omelette omeleta [ὀμελέττα]
on pano [πάνω]
   I haven't got it on me then to ekho mazee moo [δέν τό ἔχω μαζί μου]
   on Friday teen Paraskevee [τήν Παρασκευή]
   on television steen teeleorassee [στήν τηλεόραση]
once meea fora [μιά φορά]
   at once amessos [ἀμέσως]
one enas [ἕνας]
   the red one to kokeeno [τό κόκκινο]
onion ena kremeethee [ἕνα κρεμύδι]
only mono [μόνο]
open *(adjective)* aneekta [ἀνοικτά]
   I can't open it then boro na to aneexo [δέν μπορῶ νά τό ἀνοίξω]; **when do you open?** pote aneegete? [πότε ἀνοίγετε;]
opera ee opera [ἡ ὄπερα]
operation engkheereessee [ἐγχείρηση]
   will I need an operation? tha khreeassto engkheereessee? [θά χρειαστῶ ἐγχείρηση;]
operator *(telephone)* o teelefoneetees [ὁ τηλεφωνητής]
opposite apenandee [ἀπέναντι]
   opposite the hotel apenandee apo to ksenothokheeo [ἀπέναντι ἀπό τό ξενοδοχεῖο]
optician o opteekos [ὁ ὀπτικός]
or ee [ἤ]
orange portokalee [πορτοκάλι]
   orange juice kheemos portokaleeoo [χυμός πορτοκαλιοῦ]
order: could we order now? boroome na parangeelome tora? [μπορεῖτε νά παραγγείλωμε τώρα;]

thank you, we've already ordered efkhareesto ekhome eethee parangeelee [εὐχαριστῶ ἔχομε ἤδη παραγγείλει]

other: the other one to alo [τό ἄλλο]
do you have any others? ekhete teepote ala? [ἔχετε τίποτε ἄλλα;]

otherwise theeaforeteeka [διαφορετικά]

ought: I ought to go prepee na feego [πρέπει νά φύγω]

ounce oogeea [οὐγγιά]
» TRAVEL TIP: 1 ounce = 28.35 grammes

our: our hotel to ksenothokheeo mas [τό ξενοδοχεῖο μας]; **that's ours** afto eene theeko mas [αὐτό εἶναι δικό μας]

out: we're out of petrol meename apo venzeenee [μείναμε ἀπό βενζίνη]
get out! v-yes exo! [βγές ἔξω!]

outboard exolemveeos [ἐξωλέμβιος]

outdoors exo [ἔξω]

outside: can we sit outside? boroome na katheesoome exo? [μπορούμε νά καθίσουμε ἔξω;]

over: over here/there etho/ekee [ἐδῶ/ἐκεῖ]
over 40 pano apo saranda [πάνω ἀπό 40]
it's all over ola teleeossan [ὅλα τελείωσαν]

overboard: man overboard! anthropos stee thalassa [ἄνθρωπος στή θάλασσα]

overcharge: you've overcharged me me khreossate parapano [μέ χρεώσατε παραπάνω]

overcooked parapseemeno [παραψημένο]

overexposed para-ektetheemeno [παραεκτεθειμένο]

overnight (stay, travel) theeaneekterefssee [διανυκτέρευση]

oversleep parakeemame [παρακοιμᾶμαι]
I overslept parakeemeetheeka [παρακοιμήθηκα]

overtake prosperno [προσπερνῶ]

owe: what do I owe you? possa sas khrosstao? [πόσα σᾶς χρωστάω;]

own: my own ... theeko moo [δικό μου]
  are you on your own? eesse monos soo? [εἶσαι
  μόνος σου;]; **I'm on my own** eeme monos moo
  [εἶμαι μόνος μου]

owner o eetheeokteetees [ὁ ἰδιοκτήτης]

oxygen to oxeegono [τό ὀξυγόνο]

oyster to streethee [τό στρείδι]

pack: I haven't packed yet then ekana tees
  valeetses moo akoma [δέν ἔκανα τίς βαλίτσες
  μου ἀκόμα]
  can I have a packed lunch? boroome na
  paroome paketareesmeno fageeto? [μπορούμε
  νά πάρουμε πακεταρισμένο φαγητό;]

package tour omatheekee ekthromee [ὁμαδική
  ἐκδρομή]

page *(of book)* ee seleetha [ἡ σελίδα]
  could you page him? boreete na ton fonaxete
  apo to megafono? [μπορεῖτε νά τόν φωνάξετε
  ἀπό τό μεγάφωνο;]

pain o ponos [ὁ πόνος]
  I've got a pain in my chest ekho ena pono sto
  steethos moo [ἔχω ἕνα πόνο στό στῆθος μου]
  pain-killers pafsseepona [παυσίπονα]

painting ee zografeekee [ἡ ζωγραφική]

Pakistan Pakeestan [Πακιστάν]

Pakistani Pakeestanos [Πακιστανός]

pale khlomos [χλωμός]

pancake teeganeeta [τηγανίτα]

panties ee keelotes [οἱ κυλόττες]

pants pantaloneea [πανταλόνια]
  (underpants) to sleepakee [τό σλιπάκι]

paper khartee [χαρτί]
  (newspaper) efeemereetha [ἐφημερίδα]

parcel ena paketo [ἕνα πακέτο]

pardon? *(didn't understand)* seegnomee?
  [συγγνώμη;]
  I beg your pardon *(sorry)* me seenkhoreete
  [μέ συγχωρεῖτε]

parents: my parents ee gonees moo [οἱ γονεῖς
  μου]

park to parko [τό πάρκο]
  where can I park my car? poo boro na
  parkaro to aftokeeneeto moo? [πού μπορῶ νά
  παρκάρω τό αὐτοκίνητό μου;]
part meros [μέρος]
partner o seeneteros [ὁ συνέταιρος]
party (group) ee omatha [ἡ ὁμάδα]
  (celebration) to partee [τό πάρτυ]
  I'm with the ... party eeme me teen ...
  omatha [εἶμαι μέ τήν ... ὁμάδα]
pass (mountain) perasma [πέρασμα]
  he's passed out leepotheemeesse
  [λιποθύμησε]
passable (road) theeavatos [διαβατός]
passenger o epeevatees [ὁ ἐπιβάτης]
passer-by o theeavatees [ὁ διαβάτης]
passport to theeavateereeo [τό διαβατήριο]
past: in the past sto parelthon [στό παρελθόν]
  see time
pastry zeemee [ζύμη]
  (cake) gleekeesma [γλύκισμα]
path to monopatee [τό μονοπάτι]
patient: be patient kane eepomonee [κάνε
  ὑπομονή]
pattern skhetheeo [σχέδιο]
pavement to pezothromeeo [τό πεζοδρόμιο]
pay pleerono [πληρώνω]
  can I pay, please? boro na pleerosso
  parakalo? [μπορῶ νά πληρώσω παρακαλῶ;]
» TRAVEL TIP: you normally pay when you leave not
  when you order your drinks etc
peace eereenee [Εἰρήνη]
peach ena rothakeeno [ἕνα ροδάκινο]
peanuts feessteekeea arapeeka [φυστίκια
  ἀράπικα]
pear ena akhlathee [ἕνα ἀχλάδι]
peas beezeleea [μπιζέλια]
pebble khaleekee [χαλίκι]
pedal to peethalee [τό πηδάλι]
pedestrian o pezos [ὁ πεζός]

pedestrian crossing thee*a*vasse pezon
[διάβαση πεζών]
» *TRAVEL TIP: don't assume that cars will always
stop for you!*
peg *e*na mandal*a*kee [ένα μανταλάκι]
pelvis ee lek*a*nee [ἡ λεκάνη]
pen *e*na steel*o* [ένα στυλό]
  have you got a pen? *e*khete *e*na steel*o*? [ἔχετε
ένα στυλό;]
pencil *e*na mol*e*evee [ένα μολύβι]
penfriend f*ee*los thee aleelografee*a*s [φίλος δι'
ἀλληλογραφίας]
penicillin peneekeel*ee*nee [πενικιλλίνη]
penknife o soog*e*e*a*s [ὁ σουγιάς]
pensioner seendaxee*oo*khos [συνταξιοῦχος]
people *a*nthropee [ἄνθρωποι]
  the Greek people o Eleeneekos la*o*s
[ὁ Ἑλληνικός λαός]
pepper to peep*e*ree [τό πιπέρι]
  (vegetable) mee*a* peeperee*a* [μιά πιπεριά]
peppermint m*e*nta [μέντα]
per: per night/week/person to vr*a*thee/teen
evthom*a*tha/to *a*tomo [τό βράδυ/τήν
ἑβδομάδα/τό ἄτομο]
per cent tees ekat*o* [τοῖς ἑκατό]
perfect t*e*leeos [τέλειος]
  the perfect holiday ee eethaneek*e*s
theeakop*e*s [οἱ ἰδανικές διακοπές]
perfume *a*roma [ἄρωμα]
perhaps *ee*ssos [ἴσως]
period *(also medical)* pereeothos [περίοδος]
perm perman*a*nt [περμανάντ]
permit *(noun)* ath*e*ea [ἄδεια]
person *a*tomo [ἄτομο]
  in person prossop*ee*ka [προσωπικά]
petrol venz*ee*nee [βενζίνη]
  petrol station venz*ee*nee [βενζίνη]
» *TRAVEL TIP:* apl*ee* [`απλή] *is 2 star;* so*u*per
[σούπερ] *is 3 or 4 star*
philosopher *e*nas feelossofos [ἔνας φιλόσοφος]

....

photograph mee*a* fotografee*a* [μιά φωτογραφία]
would you take a photograph of us? boreete
na mas vg*a*lete mee*a* fotografee*a*? [μπορείτε νά
μᾶς βγάλετε μιά φωτογραφία;]
piano pee*a*no [πιάνο]
pickpocket en*a*s portofol*a*s [ἕνας πορτοφολάς]
picture mee*a* eek*o*na [μιά εἰκόνα]
pie pee*t*a [πίτα]
piece *e*na kom*a*tee [ἕνα κομμάτι]
a piece of . . . *e*na kom*a*tee ap*o* . . . [ἕνα
κομμάτι ἀπό . . .]
pig *e*na gooroonee [ἕνα γουρούνι]
pigeon *e*na pereesteree [ἕνα περιστέρι]
pile-up karab*o*la [καραμπόλα]
pill to kh*a*pee [τό χάπι]
do you take the pill? pernees to kh*a*pee?
[παίρνεις τό χάπι;]
pillion ee s*e*la [ἡ σέλλα]
on the pillion p*a*no stee s*e*la [πάνω στή σέλλα]
pillow *e*na maxeel*a*ree [ἕνα μαξιλάρι]
pin mee*a* karf*e*etssa [μιά καρφίτσα]
pineapple en*a*s anan*a*s [ἕνας ἀνανᾶς]
pint mee*a* peent*a* [μιά πίντα]
» *TRAVEL TIP: 1 pint = 0.57 litres*
pink roz [ρόζ]
pipe ee pee*pa* [ἡ πίπα]
pipe tobacco kap*no*s pee*pa*s [καπνός πίπας]
piston to peesst*o*nee [τό πιστόνι]
pity: it's a pity *ee*ne kreema [εἶναι κρίμα]
place m*e*ros [μέρος]
is this place taken? *ee*ne peeasmenee aft*ee* ee
*the*ssee? [εἶναι πιασμένη αὐτή ἡ θέση;]
do you know any good places to go? ks*e*rete
teepote kal*a* m*e*ree na p*a*o? [ξέρετε τίποτε καλά
μέρη νά πάω;]
plain *(not patterned)* okhee garneer*ee*smeno [ὄχι
γαρνιρισμένο]
plain food apl*o* fageet*o* [ἁπλό φαγητό]
plane to a-eropl*a*no [τό ἀεροπλάνο]
by plane a-eroporeek*o*s [ἀεροπορικῶς]

plant to feet*o* [τό φυτό]
plaster *(medical)* o yee-pss*o*s [ό γύψος]
  see **sticking**
plastic plasteek*o* [πλαστικό]
plate *e*na pee*a*t*o* [ἕνα πιάτο]
platform platf*o*rma [πλατφόρμα]
  which platform please? pee*a* platf*o*rma
  parakal*o*? [ποιά πλατφόρμα παρακαλῶ;]
pleasant efkh*a*reest*o*s [εὐχάριστος]
please: could you please . . .? parakal*o*,
  bor*e*ete . . .? [παρακαλῶ, μπορεῖτε . . .;]
  (yes) please ne parakal*o* [ναί παρακαλῶ]
pleasure efkh*a*re*e*steess*e*e [εὐχαρίστηση]
  it's a pleasure kh*a*ra mas [χαρά μας]
plenty: plenty of . . . pol*a* ap*o* . . . [πολλά
  ἀπό . . .]
  thank you, that's plenty efkh*a*reest*o* aft*o*
  *e*ene arket*o* [εὐχαριστῶ αὐτό εἶναι ἀρκετό]
pliers me*e*a p*e*nssa [μιά πένσα]
plonk *(wine)* kak*e*es pee*o*teet*a*s krass*e*e [κακής
  ποιότητας κρασί]
plug *(electrical)* ee pr*e*ez*a* [ή πρίζα]
  (car) to booz*e*e [τό μπουζί]
  (sink) tap*a* [τάπα]
plum *e*na thamask*e*eno [ἕνα δαμάσκηνο]
plumber eethr*a*vleek*o*s [ύδραβλικός]
plus seen [σύν]
p.m. meta mess*e*emvre*e*a [μ.μ. μετά
  μεσημβρία]
pneumonia pnevmon*e*ea [πνευμονία]
poached egg avg*o* poss*e* [αὐγό ποσέ]
pocket ee ts*e*pee [ή τσέπη]
point: could you point to it? bor*e*ete na to
  th*e*exete? [μπορεῖτε νά τό δείξετε;]
  four point six t*e*ssera k*o*ma *e*xee [τέσσερα
  κόμα ἔξι]
  points *(car)* plat*e*enes [πλατίνες]
police ee asst*e*enome*e*a [ή ἀστυνομία]
  get the police eethopee-*e*este teen
  asst*e*enome*e*a [εἰδοποιήστε τήν ἀστυνομία]

policeman assteenomeekos [ἀστυνομικός]
  police station to assteenomeeko tmeema [τό
ἀστυνομικό τμῆμα]
» *TRAVEL TIP: dial 100*
polish *(noun)* verneekee [βερνίκι]
  will you polish my shoes? boreete na
ya-leessete ta papootsseea moo? [μπορεῖτε νά
γυαλίσετε τά παπούτσια μου;]
polite evgeneekos [εὐγενικός]
politics poleeteeka [πολιτικά]
polluted moleesmeno [μολυσμένο]
polythene bag meea na-eelon sakoola [μιά
νάϋλον σακούλα]
pool *(swimming)* ee peesseena [ἡ πισίνα]
poor: I'm very poor eeme polee ftokhos [εἶμαι
πολύ φτωχός]
  poor quality kakee peeotees [κακή ποιότης]
popular theemofeelees [δημοφιλής]
population o pleetheesmos [ὁ πληθυσμός]
pork kheereeno [χοιρινό]
port to leemanee [τό λιμάνι]
  (drink) port [πόρτ]
  to port areessteree plevra too pleeoo [ἀριστερή
πλευρά τοῦ πλοίου]
porter o akh-thoforos [ὁ ἀχθοφόρος]
portrait to portreto [τό πορτρέτο]
posh poleetelees [πολυτελής]
possible peethano [πιθανό]
  could you possibly . . .? tha sas eetan
theenaton na . . .? [θά σᾶς ἦταν δυνατό νά . . .;]
post takheethromo [ταχυδρομῶ]
  postcard ee karta [ἡ κάρτα]
  post office to takheethromeeo [τό
ταχυδρομεῖο]
» *TRAVEL TIP: letter boxes are yellow; stamps can
also be bought at tobacconists, kiosks and
sometimes ironmongers*
poste resante post restand
[πόστ-ρεστάντ]
potato ee patata [ἡ πατάτα]

pottery kerameek*a* [κεραμικά]
pound ee leetra [ή λίτρα]
(*money*) ee leer*a* [ή λίρα]

» TRAVEL TIP: conversion: $\dfrac{pounds}{11} \times 5 = kilos$

pounds	1	3	5	6	7	8	9
kilos	0.45	1.4	2.3	2.7	3.2	3.6	4.1

pour: it's pouring vrekhe pol*ee* [βρέχει πολύ]
powder ee p*oo*thra [ή πούδρα]
power cut theeakop*ee* revmatos [διακοπή ρεύματος]
power point ee preez*a* [ή πρίζα]
prawns gar*ee*thes [γαρίδες]
prefer: I prefer this one proteem*o* aft*o* [προτιμῶ αὐτό]
pregnant engheeos [ἔγκυος]
prescription mee*a* seentag*ee* [μιά συνταγή]
present: at present pros to par*on* [πρός τό παρόν]
here's a present for you aft*o* eene ena thoro ya sena [αὐτό εἶναι ἕνα δῶρο γιά σένα]
president o pro-ethros [ὁ πρόεδρος]
press: could you press these? boreete na seetherossete aft*a*? [μπορεῖτε νά σιδερώσετε αὐτά;]
pretty orea [ὡραία]
pretty good pol*ee* kal*o* [πολύ καλό]
price ee teem*ee* [ή τιμή]
priest o pap*a*s [ὁ παππᾶς]
printed matter teepomeno eeleeko [τυπωμένο ὑλικό]
prison ee feelak*ee* [ή φυλακή]
private eetheeoteekos [ἰδιωτικός]
probably pee*th*anos [πιθανῶς]
problem ena provleema [ἕνα πρόβλημα]
product pro-ee-on [προϊόν]
profit to k*e*rthos [τό κέρδος]
promise: do you promise? eeposkhesse? [ὑπόσχεσαι;]
I promise eeposkhome [ὑπόσχομαι]

pronounce: how do you pronounce this? pos to prof*ee*rees afto? [πῶς τό προφέρεις αὐτό;]

propeller ee prop*e*la [ἡ προπέλλα]

properly *o*pos prep*ee* [ὅπως πρέπει]

property eetheeokt*ee*ss*ee*a [ἰδιοκτησία]

prostitute ee porn*ee* [ἡ πόρνη]

protect prosst*a*tevo [προστατεύω]

Protestant Protest*a*ndees [Προτεστάντης]

proud eeper*ee*fanos [ὑπερήφανος]

prove: I can prove it boro na to apoth*ee*xo [μπορῶ νά τό ἀποδείξω]

public: the public to k*ee*no [τό κοινό]
  public convenience theem*o*sseea tooal*e*ta [δημόσια τουαλέττα]

» *TRAVEL TIP: public conveniences are extremely few and far between; but it's quite usual to use the toilet in bars, cafes, restaurants, hotels without asking*

» *TRAVEL TIP: Public Holidays*
  1 January Protokhron*ee*a [Πρωτοχρονιά] *New Year's Day*
  6 January Theof*a*neea [Θεοφάνεια] *Epiphany*
  25 March *Eth*neek*ee* Eort*ee* ['Εθνική 'Εορτή] *National Day*
  Meg*a*lee Parask*e*vee [Μεγάλη Παρασκευή] *Good Friday*
  Meg*a*lo S*a*vato [Μεγάλο Σάββατο] *Easter Saturday*
  P*a*skha [Πάσχα] *Easter*
  1 May Ergat*ee*k*ee* eort*ee* ['Εργατική 'Εορτή] *Labour Day*
  15 August Keem*ee*ss*ee* tees Theot*o*koo [Κοίμηση τῆς Θεοτόκου] *Assumption*
  28 October *Eth*neek*ee* eort*ee* ['Εθνική 'Εορτή] *National Day*
  25 December Khreest*o*ogena [Χριστούγεννα] *Christmas*
  26 December S*ee*naxee Theot*o*koo [Σύναξη Θεοτόκου] *Boxing Day*

pudding poot*ee*ngha [πουτίγγα]

pull *(verb)* travo [τραβῶ]
   he pulled out in front of me pet*a*khteeke
   brosta moo [πετάχτηκε μπροστά μου]
pump ee andl*ee*a [ἡ ἀντλία]
punctual: he is very punctual *ee*ne p*a*nda
   steen or*a* too [εἶναι πάντα στήν ὥρα του]
puncture me*ea* treep*a* sto last*ee*kho [μιά τρύπα
   στό λάστιχο]
pure agn*os* [ἀγνός]
purple mov [μώβ]
purse to portofol*ee* [τό πορτοφόλι]
push *(verb)* sprokhno [σπρώχνω]
   don't push m*ee* sprokhnees [μή σπρώχνεις]
   push-chair karotss*a*kee [καροτσάκι]
put: where can I put . . .? poo boro na val*o* . . .?
   [ποῦ μπορῶ νά βάλω . . .;]
pyjamas ee peetz*a*mes [οἱ πυτζάμες]
quality ee pe*eo*tees [ἡ ποιότης]
quarantine ee karant*ee*na [ἡ καραντίνα]
quarter ena tetarto [ἕνα τέταρτο]
   a quarter of an hour *e*na tetarto tees*o*ras [ἕνα
   τέταρτο τῆς ὥρας]
quay ee provl*ee*ta [ἡ προβλήτα]
question me*ea* eroteessee [μιά ἐρώτηση]
» *TRAVEL TIP: orderly queuing is not so widespread*
  as in the UK
quick greegor*a* [γρήγορα]; **that was quick** afto
  *ee*tan greegor*o* [αὐτό ἦταν γρήγορο]
quiet *ee*sseekha [ἥσυχα]
   be quiet! seeop*ee*! [σιωπή!]
quite endel*os* [ἐντελῶς]
   (fairly) arket*a* [ἀρκετά]
   quite a lot pol*a* [πολλά]
radiator *(car)* pseeg*ee*o aftokeen*ee*too [ψυγεῖο
   αὐτοκινήτου]
   (heater) to kaloreef*er* [τό καλοριφέρ]
radio to rath*ee*ofono [τό ραδιόφωνο]
rail: by rail seetheerothrom*ee*k*os*
   [σιδηροδρομικῶς]

rain ee vrokh*ee* [ἡ βροχή]
   it's raining vr*e*khee [βρέχει]
   raincoat ee kabard*ee*na [ἡ καμπαρντίνα]
rally *(car)* ra*lee* [ράλυ]
rape veeasm*os* [βιασμός]
rare spa*nee*os [σπάνιος]
   (steak) o*kh*ee pol*ee* pseem*e*no [ὄχι πολύ ψημένο]
raspberry vato*moo*ro [βατόμουρο]
rat *e*nas aroor*e*os [ἕνας ἀρουραῖος]
rather: I'd rather sit here prote*e*mo na
   ka*thee*sso etho [προτιμῶ νά καθήσω ἐδῶ]
   I'd rather not then *that*ela [δέν θἄθελα]
   it's rather hot *ee*ne ma*lon zesto [εἶναι μᾶλλον
   ζεστό]
raw om*o* [ὠμό]
razor kseera*fee* [ξυράφι]
   razor blades kseerafa*kee*a [ξυραφάκια]
read: you read it thee*a*vaze to ess*ee* [διάβαζέ το
   ἐσύ]
   something to read ka*tee* na thee*a*vasso [κάτι
   νά διαβάσω]
ready: when will it be ready? pote *tha* eene
   eteem*o*? [πότε θά εἶναι ἕτοιμο;]
   I'm not ready yet then *ee*me *e*teemos ako*mee*
   [δέν εἶμαι ἕτοιμος ἀκόμη]
real pragmatee*kos* [πραγματικός]
really pragmatee*ka* [πραγματικά]
rear-view mirror ka*thr*eftees aftokeen*ee*too
   [καθρέφτης αὐτοκινήτου]
reasonable logee*kos* [λογικός]
receipt apothe*exee* [ἀπόδειξη]
   can I have a receipt, please? bor*ee*te na moo
   th*o*ssete m*ee*a apothe*exee*, parakalo? [μπορεῖτε
   νά μου δώσετε μία ἀπόδειξη, παρακαλῶ;]
recently prossfata [πρόσφατα]
reception *(hotel)* ee ressepse*eon* [ἡ ρεσεψιόν]
   at reception stee ressepse*eon* [στήν ρεσεψιόν]
receptionist ee ressepssee*on*eest
   [ἡ ρεσεψιονίστ]
recipe ee seendag*ee* [ἡ συνταγή]

recommend: can you recommend . . .?
boreete na moo seessteessete . . .? [μπορείτε
νά μοῦ συστήσετε . . .;]
record *(music)* o theeskos [ό δίσκος]
red kokkeeno [κόκκινο]
reduction *(in price)* ekptossee [ἔκπτωση]
refuse: I refuse arnoome [ἀρνοῦμαι]
region ee pereefereea [ή περιφέρεια]
in this region saftee teen pereefereea [σ' αὐτή
τήν περιφέρεια]
registered letter seesteemeno grama
[συστημένο γράμμα]
regret leepoome [λυποῦμαι]
I have no regrets then metaneeossa katholoo
[δέν μετάνοιωσα καθόλου]
relax: I just want to relax thelo na eeremeesso
mono [θέλω νά ἠρεμήσω μόνο]
relax! eeremeesse! [ἠρέμησε!]
remember: don't you remember? then
theemassee? [δέν θυμᾶσαι;]
I'll always remember tha theemame panda
[θά θυμᾶμαι πάντα]
something to remember you by katee geea
na se theemame [κάτι γιά νά σέ θυμᾶμαι]
rent: can I rent a car/boat/bicycle? boro na
neekeeasso ena aftokeeneeto/meea varka/ena
potheelato? [μπορῶ νά νοικιάσω ἕνα
αὐτοκίνητο/μιά βάρκα/ἕνα ποδήλατο;]
repair: can you repair it? borete na to
epeeskevassete? [μπορεῖτε νά τό ἐπισκευάσετε;]
repeat: could you repeat that? boreete na to
epanalavete? [μπορεῖτε νά τό ἐπαναλάβετε;]
reputation ee feemee [ή φήμη]
rescue *(verb)* sozo [σώζω]
reservation krateessee thesseos [κράτηση
θέσεως]
I want to make a reservation for . . . thelo na
krateesso thessees geea . . . [θέλω νά κρατήσω
θέσεις γιά . . .]
reserve: can I reserve a seat? boro na kleesso

mee*a the*ssee? [μπορῶ νά κλείσω μιά θέση;]

responsible eepef*th*eenos [ὑπεύθυνος]

rest: I've come here for a rest ee*r*tha etho gee*a*
na ksekoorasto [ἦρθα ἐδῶ γιά νά ξεκουραστῶ]
you keep the rest krat*ee*ste ta eepoleepa
[κρατῆστε τά ὑπόλοιπα]

restaurant to esteeatoreeo [τό ἐστιατόριο]

retired seendaxee*o*okhos [συνταξιοῦχος]

return: a return/two returns to . . . me
epeestrof*ee*/th*ee*o me epeestrof*ee* [μέ
ἐπιστροφή/δύο μέ ἐπιστροφή]

reverse gear opeess*th*en [ὄπισθεν]

rheumatism revmatees*m*ee [ρευματισμοί]

Rhodes Rothos [Ρόδος]

rib ee plevr*a* [ἡ πλευρά]

rice ree*z*ee [ρύζι]

rich *(person, food)* ploosseeos [πλούσιος]

ridiculous ye-l*ee*os [γελεῖος]

right: that's right sosst*a* [σωστά]
you're right ekhees the*k*eeo [ἔχεις δίκιο]
on the right sta thexee*a* [στά δεξιά]
right now tora am*e*ssos [τώρα ἀμέσως]
right here etho [ἐδῶ]
righthand drive me thexee*o* teem*o*nee [μέ
δεξιό τιμόνι]

ring *(on finger)* to thakteel*ee*thee [τό δακτυλίδι]

ripe oreemos [ὥριμος]

rip-off: it's a rip-off ee*n*e leessteea [εἶναι
ληστεία]

river to potamee [τό ποτάμι]

road o thromos [ὁ δρόμος]
which is the road to . . .? pee*o*s ee*n*e o
thromos pros . . .? [ποιός εἶναι ὁ δρόμος
πρός . . .;]
roadhog adzam*ee*s otheego*s* [ἀτζαμής ὁδηγός]

rob: I've been robbed me l*ee*stepsan [μέ
λήστευσαν]

rock o bra*k*hos [ὁ βράχος]
whisky on the rocks whisky me paga*k*eea
[οὐΐσκι μέ παγάκια]

roll *(bread)* ena psomakee [ἕνα ψωμάκι]
Roman Catholic Katholeekos [Καθολικός]
romantic romandeekos [ρομαντικός]
roof ee orofee [ἡ ὀροφή]
room to thomateeo [τό δωμάτιο]

have you got a (single/double) room?
ekhete ena mono/theplo thomateeo? [ἔχετε ἕνα
μονό/διπλό δωμάτιο;]

for one night/for three nights geea meea
vratheea/geea trees vrathee-es [γιά μιά
βραδιά/γιά τρεῖς βραδιές]

YOU MAY THEN HEAR...

then ekhome *we're full up*
me baneeo ee me khorees baneeo? *with bath or
without bath?*
ekhome mono geea ... brathee-es *only
for ... nights*

room service servees thomateeoo [σέρβις
δωματίου]
rope to skheenee [τό σχοινί]
rose to treeandafeelo [τό τριαντάφυλο]
rough *(person)* agreekos [ἀγροῖκος]
(sea) treekeemeeothess [τρικυμιώδης]
roughly *(approximately)* pano kato [πάνω κάτω]
roulette rooleta [ρουλέττα]
round *(circular)* strogheelos [στρογγυλός]
roundabout plateea [πλατεία]
» *TRAVEL TIP: be careful, cars on a roundabout
don't have priority*
route poreea [πορεία]

which is the prettiest/fastest route? peeos
eene peeo oreos/peeo seendomos thromos? [ποιός
εἶναι ποιό ὡραῖος/ποιό σύντομος δρόμος;]

rowing boat meea varka me koopeea [μιά βάρκα
μέ κουπιά]
rubber lassteekho [λάστιχο]
rubberband ena lasstekhakee [ἕνα
λαστιχάκι]
rubbish *(garbage)* skoopeetheea [σκουπίδια]
rubbish! treekhes! [τρίχες!]

rucksack o sakos [ὁ σάκος]
rudder to peethalee [τό πηδάλι]
rude agenees [ἀγενής]
ruin ereepeeo [ἐρείπιο]
rum roomee [ρούμι]

  rum and coke roomee me koka-kola [ρούμι μέ κόκα-κόλα]

run: hurry, run! veeassoo, trexe [βιάσου, τρέξε]
  I've run out of petrol/money emeena apo venzeenee/lefta [ἔμεινα ἀπό βενζίνη/λεφτά]
sad leepeemenos [λυπημένος]
safe asfales [ἀσφαλές]
  will it be safe here? thaeene asfales etho? [θά εἶναι ἀσφαλές ἐδῶ;]
  is it safe to swim here? eene asfales na koleembeesome etho? [εἶναι ἀσφαλές νά κολυμπήσωμε ἐδῶ;]
safety asfaleea [ἀσφάλεια]
  safety pin meea paramana [μιά παραμάνα]
sail (verb) taxeethevo me pleeo [ταξιδεύω μέ πλοῖο]
  can we go sailing? boroome na pame varkatha? [μποροῦμε νά πᾶμε βαρκάδα;]
sailor naftees [ναύτης]
salad meea salata [μιά σαλάτα]
salami salamee [σαλάμι]
sale: is it for sale? eene ya pooleema? [εἶναι γιά πούλημα;]
salmon o solomos [ὁ σολομός]
salt to alatee [τό ἁλάτι]
same eetheeos [ἴδιος]
  the same again, please to eetheeo ksana parakalo [τό ἴδιο ξανά παρακαλῶ]
  the same to you epeessees [ἐπίσης]
sand ee amos [ἡ ἄμμος]
sandal to santhalo [τό σάνδαλο]
sandwich ena sandwich [ἕνα σάντουϊτς]
sanitary towel servee-etes [σερβιέτες]
satisfactory eekanopee-eeteekos [ἱκανοποιητικός]

Saturday Savato [Σάββατο]
sauce saltssa [σάλτσα]
 saucepan meea katsarola [μιά κατσαρόλα]
saucer ena pee-atakee [ἕνα πιατάκι]
sauna ee saoona [ἡ σάουνα]
sausage ena lookaneeko [ἕνα λουκάνικο]
save *(life)* sozo [σώζω]
say: how do you say . . . in Greek? pos
 lene . . . sta eleeneeka? [πῶς λένε . . . στά
 Ἑλληνικά;]
 what did he say? tee eepe? [τί εἶπε;]
scarf ee sarpa [ἡ σάρπα]
scenery ee thea [ἡ θέα]
schedule to programa [τό πρόγραμμα]
 on/behind schedule steen ora too/ekhee
 katheestereessee [στήν ὥρα του/ἔχει
 καθυστέρηση]
 scheduled flight programateesmenee
 pteessee [προγραμματισμένη πτήση]
school to skholeeo [τό σχολεῖο]
scissors: a pair of scissors ena psaleethee [ἕνα
 ψαλίδι]
scooter to skooter [τό σκοῦτερ]
Scotland Skoteea [Σκωτία]
Scottish Skotsezos [Σκωτσέζος]
scratch *(noun)* meea tsagrooneea [μιά
 τσαγκρουνιά]
scream *(verb)* ksefoneezo [ξεφωνίζω]
screw *(noun)* ee veetha [ἡ βίδα]
 screwdriver ena katssaveethee [ἕνα
 κατσαβίδι]
sea ee thalassa [ἡ θάλασσα]
 by the sea konta stee thalassa [κοντά στή
 θάλασσα]
seafood thalasseena [θαλασσινά]
search *(verb)* psakhno [ψάχνω]
 search party omatha erevnees [ὁμάδα
 ἔρευνας]
seasick: I get seasick anakatevome
 [ἀνακατεύομε]

....

I feel seasick ess*tha*nome naft*ee*a [αἰσθάνομαι ναυτία]

seaside paral*ee*a [παραλία]
  let's go to the seaside p*a*me stee paral*ee*a [πᾶμε στή παραλία]

season epokh*ee* [ἐποχή]
  in the high/low season teen per*ee*odo ekhm*ee*s/nekr*ee* per*ee*odo [τήν περίοδο αἰχμῆς/νεκρή περίοδο]

seasoning bakhar*ee*k*a* [μπαχαρικά]

seat m*ee*a *the*ss*ee* [μιά θέση]
  is this somebody's seat? *ee*ne pe*ea*sm*ee*nee aft*ee* ee *the*ss*ee*? [εἶναι πιασμένη αὐτή ἡ θέση;]
  seat belt z*o*nee assfal*ee*as [ζώνη ἀσφαλείας]

sea-urchin enas akh*ee*nos [ἕνας ἀχινός]

seaweed to f*ee*kee [τό φύκι]

second *(adjective)* theftero*s* [δεύτερος]
  (time) *e*na theftero*lepto* [ἕνα δευτερόλεπτο]
  just a second m*ee*a steegm*ee* [μιά στιγμή]
  second hand theftero khr*ee*e [δεύτερο χέρι]

see vl*e*po [βλέπω]
  oh, I see ah, katalava [ἄ, κατάλαβα]
  have you seen . . .? *ee*that*e* . . .? [εἴδατε . . .;]
  can I see the room? boro na tho to thom*a*teeo? [μπορῶ νά δῶ τό δωμάτειο;]

seem: it seems so *e*tss*ee* f*e*nete [ἔτσι φαίνεται]

seldom sp*a*neea [σπάνια]

self-service self-serv*ee*s [σέλφ-σέρβις]

sell pool*o* [πουλῶ]

send st*e*lno [στέλνω]

sensitive evess*th*eetos [εὐαίσθητος]

sentimental ess*th*eematee*ko*s [αἰσθηματικός]

separate *(adjective)* khoreesto*s* [χωριστός]
  I'm separated *ee*me se the*ea*sstasee [εἶμαι σέ διάσταση]
  can we pay separately? bor*oo*me na pleerossoome khore*e*sst*a*? [μπορούμε νά πληρώσουμε χωριστά;]

September Septe*mvreeos* [Σεπτέμβριος]

serious sovaro*s* [σοβαρός]

....

I'm serious to leo sovara [τό λέω σοβαρά]
this is serious afto eene sovaro [αὐτό εἶναι σοβαρό]
is it serious, doctor? eene sovaro, ya-tre? [εἶναι σοβαρό, γιατρέ;]
service: the service was excellent/poor to servees eetan exokho/khaleea [τό σέρβις ἦταν ἔξοχο/χάλια]
　service station venzeenee [βενζίνη]
serviette meea petsseta fageetoo [μιά πετσέτα φαγητοῦ]
several mereekee [μερικοί]
sexy sexy [σέξυ]
shade: in the shade stee skeea [στή σκιά]
shake koono [κουνῶ]
　to shake hands kheerapsseea [χειραψία]
» TRAVEL TIP: customary to shake hands when you meet someone and when you leave them
shallow reekhos [ρηχός]
shame: what a shame! tee kreema! [τί κρῖμα!]
shampoo to sampooan [τό σαμπουάν]
shandy beera me lemonatha [μπύρα μέ λεμονάδα]
» TRAVEL TIP: a strange thing to ask for; don't expect it to taste like real shandy
share (room, table) meerazome [μοιράζομαι]
shark karkhareeas [καρχαρίας]
sharp koftero [κοφτερό]
shave kseereezo [ξυρίζω]
　shaver kseereesteekee meekhanee [ξυριστική μηχανή]
　shaving foam krema kseereesmatos [κρέμα ξυρίσματος]
　shaving point preeza kseereesteekees [πρίζα ξυριστικής]
she aftee [αὐτή]
　she is eene [εἶναι]
　she has left efeege [ἔφυγε]
sheep ena arnee [ἕνα ἀρνί]
sheet to sendonee [τό σεντόνι]
shelf to rafee [τό ράφι]

....

shell to keleefos [τό κέλυφος]
  shellfish *(plural)* ostrako-eethee
  [ὀστρακοειδῆ]
shelter to katafeegeeo [τό καταφύγιο]
  can we shelter here? boroome na
  profeelakhtoome etho? [μπορούμε νά
  προφυλαχτούμε ἐδῶ;]
sherry ena sherry [ἕνα σέρρυ]
ship to pleeo [τό πλοῖο]
shirt to pookameesso [τό πουκάμισο]
shock sok [σόκ]
  I got an electric shock from the . . .
  me teenaxe to revma too . . . [μέ τίναξε τό ρεῦμα
  τοῦ . . .]
  shock-absorber to amorteesser [τό
  ἀμορτισέρ]
shoe to papootssee [τό παπούτσι]
» *TRAVEL TIP: shoe sizes*

UK	4	5	6	7	8	9	10	11
Greece	37	38	39	41	42	43	44	46

shop to magazee [τό μαγαζί]
  I've some shopping to do ekho na kano
  mereeka psoneea [ἔχω νά κάνω μερικά
  ψώνια]
shore ee aktee [ἡ ἀκτή]
short kondos [κοντός]
  I'm three short moo leepoon treea [μοῦ
  λείπουν τρία . . .]
  short cut seendomos thromos [σύντομος
  δρόμος]
shorts shorts [σόρτς]
shoulder omos [ὦμος]
shout fonazo [φωνάζω]
show: please show me parakalo theexe moo
  [παρακαλῶ δεῖξε μου]
shower: with shower me doos [μέ ντούς]
shrimps gareethes [γαρίδες]
shut: it was shut eetan kleesto [ἦταν κλειστό]
  when do you shut? pote kleenete? [πότε
  κλείνετε;]

shut up! skasse! [σκάσε!]
shy dropalos [ντροπαλός]
sick arosstos [άρρωστος]
  I feel sick anakatevome [ἀνακατεύομαι]
  he's been sick ekane emeto [ἔκανε ἐμετό]
side plevra [πλευρά]
  side light fota poreeas [φῶτα πορείας]
  side street thromakee [δρομάκι]
  by the side of the road steen akree too
  thromoo [στήν ἄκρη τοῦ δρόμου]
sight: out of sight then fenete [δέν φαίνεται]
  the sights ta axeeotheata [τά ἀξιοθέατα]
  sightseeing tour ekthromee sta axeeotheata
  [ἐκδρομή στά ἀξιοθέατα]
  we'd like to go on a sightseeing tour
  thelome na pame meea ekthromee na thoome ta
  axeeotheata [θέλομε νά πᾶμε μιά ἐκδρομή νά
  δοῦμε τά ἀξιοθέατα]
sign *(notice)* ee peenakeetha [ἡ πινακίδα]
signal: he didn't signal then ekane seema [δέν
  ἔκανε σῆμα]
signature meea eepografee [μιά ὑπογραφή]
silence seeopee [σιωπή]
silencer ee exatmeessee [ἡ ἐξάτμηση]
silk metaxee [μετάξι]
silly anoeetos [ἀνόητος]
silver asseemeneeos [ἀσημένιος]
similar omeeos [ὅμοιος]
simple aplo [ἁπλό]
since: since last week apo teen perasmenee
  evthomatha [ἀπό τήν περασμένη ἑβδομάδα]
  since we arrived apo tote poo fthassame [ἀπό
  τότε πού φθάσαμε]
  (because) epeethee [ἐπειδή]
sincere eeleekreenees [εἰλικρινής]
  yours sincerely eeleekreena theekos sas
  [εἰλικρινά δικός σας]
sing tragootho [τραγουδῶ]
single monos [μόνος]
  single room mono thomateeo [μονό δωμάτιο]

I'm single *ee*me elef*th*eros [εἶμαι ἐλεύθερος]
a single to Crete *e*na ap*l*o ya teen Kree*t*ee [ἕνα ἁπλό γιά τήν Κρήτη]
sink: it sank voo*l*eeaxe [βούλιαξε]
sir k*ee*ree-e [κύριε]
sister: my sister ee athelf*ee* moo [ἡ ἀδελφή μου]
sit: can I sit here? boro na ka*t*sso e*th*o [μπορῶ νά κάτσω ἐδῶ]
size m*eget*hos [μέγεθος]
skid gleestro [γλυστρῶ]
skin *th*erma [δέρμα]
    skin-diving eepov*ree*kheea kata*th*eessee [ὑποβρύχια κατάδυση]
» *TRAVEL TIP: use of an aqualung requires a permit from the police*
skirt ee foosta [ἡ φούστα]
sky o ooranos [ὁ οὐρανός]
sleep: I can't sleep the*n* boro na keem*eet*ho [δέν μπορῶ νά κοιμηθῶ]
    sleeper *(rail)* vagon lee [βαγκόν λή]
    sleeping bag 'sleeping bag' [σλίπινγκ μπάγκ]
    sleeping pill eepno*t*eeko khapee [ὑπνοτικό χάπι]
    YOU MAY HEAR ...
    kee*m*ee*th*eekes kala? *did you have a good sleep?*
sleeve to man*ee*kee [τό μανίκι]
slide *(phot)* to 'slide' [τό σλάϊντ]
slow arga [ἀργά]; **could you speak a little slower?** bor*ee*te na meela*t*e pe*e*o arga? [μπορεῖτε νά μηλᾶτε πιό ἀργά;]
small meekro [μικρό]
    small change pseela [ψιλά]
smell: there's a funny smell meer*ee*zee per*ee*-erga [μυρίζει περίεργα]
    it smells vroma*ee*e [βρωμάει]
smile *(verb)* khamogelo [χαμογελῶ]
smoke *(noun)* to ka*p*neezma [τό κάπνισμα]
    do you smoke? kap*n*eezete? [καπνίζετε;]
    can I smoke? boro na kapn*ee*sso? [μπορῶ νά καπνίσω;]

smooth apalos [ἁπαλός]
snack: can we just have a snack? boroome na tsseebeessome katee? [μπορούμε νά τσιμπήσομε κάτι;]
snorkel enas anapnefsteeras [ἕνας ἀναπνευστήρας]
snow kheeonee [χιόνι]
so: it's so hot today kanee tosse zesstee seemera [κάνει τόση ζέστη σήμερα]
 not so much okhee tosso polee [ὄχι τόσο πολύ]
 so-so etssee ke etssee [ἔτσι καί ἔτσι]
soap ena sapoonee [ἕνα σαπούνι]
 soap powder aporeepandeeko [ἀπορυπαντικό]
sober ksemetheestos [ξεμέθυστος]
sock meea kaltssa [μιά κάλτσα]
soda (water) sotha [σόδα]
soft drink ena mee alko-oleeko poto [ἕνα μή ἀλκοολικό ποτό]
sole (of shoe) sola [σόλα]
 (fish) glossa [γλῶσσα]
 could you put new soles on these? boreete na moo valete kenoorgee-es soles safta? [μπορεῖτε νά βάλετε καινούργιες σόλες σ' αὐτά;]
some: some people mereekee anthropee [μερικοί ἄνθρωποι]
 can I have some? boro naekho leega? [μπορῶ νά ἔχω λίγα;]
 can I have some grapes/some bread? boro na ekho leega stafeeleea/leego psomee? [μπορῶ νά ἔχω λίγα σταφύλια/λίγο ψωμί;]
 can I have some more? boro na ekho leego akomee? [μπορῶ νά ἔχω λίγο ἀκόμη;]
 that's some drink! afto eene poto! [αὐτό εἶναι ποτό!]
somebody kapeeos [κάποιος]
something katee [κάτι]
sometime kambossee ora [κάμποση ὥρα]
 sometimes kameea fora [καμιά φορά]
somewhere kapoo [κάπου]

son: my son o yee-os moo [ὁ γιός μου]
song to tragoothee [τό τραγούδι]
soon seentoma [σύντομα]
    as soon as possible osso to theenato
    seendomotera [ὅσο τό δυνατό συντομώτερα]
    sooner peeo norees [πιό νωρίς]
sore: it's sore ponaee [πονάει]
    sore throat ponolemos [πονόλεμος]
sorry: (I'm) sorry leepame [λυπάμαι]
sort: this sort afto to eethos [αὐτό τό εἶδος]
    what sort of . . .? tee eethos . . .? [τί
    εἶδος . . .;]
    will you sort it out? tha to kanoneessees? [θά
    τό κανονίσεις;]
soup soopa [σούπα]
sour kseeno [ξυνό]
south o notos [ὁ νότος]
South Africa Noteeos Afreekee [Νότιος
    'Αφρική]
South African NoteeoAfreekanos
    [ΝοτιοΑφρικανός]
souvenir ena entheemeeo [ἕνα ἐνθύμιο]
spade ena fteearee [ἕνα φτιάρι]
spanner ena kleethee [ἕνα κλειδί]
spare: spare part andalakteeko
    [ἀνταλλακτικό]
    spare wheel ee rezerva [ἡ ρεζέρβα]
spark(ing) plug to boozee [τό μπουζί]
speak: do you speak English? meelate
    agleeka? [μιλάτε 'Αγγλικά;]
    I don't speak . . . then meelo . . . [δέν
    μιλῶ . . .]
special eethee-eteros [ἰδιαίτερος]
specialist eetheekos [εἰδικός]
specially eethee-eteros [ἰδιαιτέρως]
spectacles ta yee-aleea [τά γυαλιά]
speed ee takheetees [ἡ ταχύτης]
    he was speeding etrekhe [ἕτρεχε]
    speed limit oreeo takheeteetos [ὅριο
    ταχύτητος]

speedometer to konter [τό κοντέρ]
  see **driving**
spend *(money)* ksothevo [ξοδεύω]
spice bakhareeko [μπαχαρικό]
  is it spicy? ekhee bakhareeka? [ἔχει
  μπαχαρικά;]
  it's too spicy ekhee polla bakhareeka [ἔχει
  πολλά μπαχαρικά]
spider meea arakhnee [μιά ἀράχνη]
spirits *(drink)* alko-oleeka pota [ἀλκοολικά
  ποτά]
spoon ena kootalee [ἕνα κουτάλι]
sprain: I've sprained it to strambooleexa [τό
  στραμπούληξα]
spring ee peegee [ἡ πηγή]
  (season) aneexee [ἄνοιξη]
square *(in town)* ee plateea [ἡ πλατεῖα]
  2 square metres theeo tetragoneeka metra
  [δύο τετραγωνικά μέτρα]
stairs ee skales [οἱ σκάλες]
stale bayateeko [μπαγιάτικο]
stalls plateea [πλατεῖα]
stamp ena grammatosseemo [ἕνα
  γραμματόσημο]
  two stamps for England theeo
  grammatosseema ya teen Angleea [δύο
  γραμματόσημα γιά τήν 'Αγγλία]
standard standard [στάνταρ]
star to asstro [τό ἄστρο]
starboard thexeea plevra pleeoo [δεξιά πλευρά
  πλοίου]
start ksekeeno [ξεκινῶ]
  my car won't start to aftokeeneeto moo then
  ksekeenaee [τό αὐτοκίνητό μου δέν ξεκινάει]
  when does it start? pote arkheezee? [πότε
  ἀρχίζει;]
starter ee meeza [ἡ μίζα]
starving: I'm starving petheno tees peenas
  [πεθαίνω τῆς πείνας]
station o stathmos [ὁ σταθμός]

statue to *a*galma [τό ἄγαλμα]

stay: we enjoyed our stay theeasketh*a*ssame teen theeamon*ee* mas [διασκεδάσαμε τήν διαμονή μας]

    stay there m*ee*ne ek*ee* [μεῖνε ἐκεῖ]

    I'm staying at Hotel . . . m*e*no sto ksenothok*hee*o . . . [μένω στό ξενοδοχεῖο . . .]

steak m*ee*a breez*o*la [μιά μπριζόλα]

    YOU MAY HEAR . . .

    pos t*ee* thel*e*te? *how would you like it done?*

    kal*a* pseem*e*nee? *well done?*

    ok*he*e pol*ee* pseem*e*nee? *rare?*

» *TRAVEL TIP: a rare steak will be very rare!*

steep apot*o*mo [ἀπότομο]

steering to s*ee*steema thee-*e*fth*ee*nsees [τό σύστημα διεύθυνσης]

    steering wheel to teem*o*nee [τό τιμόνι]

step *(noun)* to skal*ee* [τό σκαλί]

stereo stereofon*ee*ko seengrot*ee*ma [στερεοφωνικό συγκρότημα]

sterling ee sterl*ee*na [ἡ στερλίνα]

stewardess ee a-erossee*no*thos [ἡ ἀεροσυνοδός]

sticking plaster lefkopl*a*st [λευκοπλάστ]

sticky koloth*ee*s [κολλώδης]

stiff al*ee*-yeestos [ἀλύγιστος]

still: keep still st*a*ssoo ak*ee*neetos [στάσου ἀκίνητος]; **I'm still here** *ee*me akomee eth*o* [εἶμαι ἀκόμη ἐδώ]

stink *(noun)* br*o*ma [βρῶμα]

stolen: my wallet's been stolen moo kl*e*psane to portof*o*lee [μοῦ κλέψανε τό πορτοφόλι]

stomach to stom*a*khee [τό στομάχι]

    I have stomach-ache pona*ee* to stom*a*khee moo [πονάει τό στομάχι μου]

    have you got something for an upset stomach? ekhete kanena f*a*rmako ya p*o*no stomakhe*oo*? [ἔχετε κανένα φάρμακο γιά πόνο στομαχιοῦ;]

stone m*ee*a petra [μιά πέτρα]

» *TRAVEL TIP: 1 stone = 6.35 kilos*

stop: stop! stamata [σταμάτα]
   stop-over stamateema [σταμάτημα]
   (overnight) theeaneekterefssee
   [διανυκτέρευση]
   do you stop near ...? stamatate konda ...?
   [σταματᾶτε κοντά ...;]
storm ee *thee*-ela [ἡ θύελλα]
straight eesseea [ἴσια]
   go straight on peegenete eesseea [πηγαίνετε
   ἴσια]
   straight away amessos [ἀμέσως]
   straight whisky sketo whisky [σκέτο οὐΐσκυ]
strange paraxenos [παράξενος]
stranger ksenos [ξένος]; **I'm a stranger**
   here eeme ksenos etho [εἶμαι ξένος ἐδῶ]
strawberry ee fraoola [ἡ φράουλα]
street o thromos [ὁ δρόμος]
string: have you got any string? ekhete
   katholoo spango? [ἔχετε καθόλου σπάγγο;]
stroke: he's had a stroke epathe prosbolee
   [ἔπαθε προσβολή]
strong theenatos [δυνατός]
student feeteetees [φοιτητής]
stung: I've been stung me tsseembeesse [μέ
   τσίμπησε]
stupid vlakas [βλάκας]
such: such a lot tosso pola [τόσο πολλά]
suddenly ksafneeka [ξαφνικά]
sugar ee zakharee [ἡ ζάχαρη]
suit *(man's)* ena koostoomee [ἕνα κουστούμι]
   (woman's) to tayer [τό ταγιέρ]
   suitcase ee valeedza [ἡ βαλίτσα]
suitable kataleelos [κατάλληλος]
summer to kalokeree [τό καλοκαίρι]
sun o eeleeos [ὁ ἥλιος]
   in the sun ston eeleeo [στόν ἥλιο]
   out of the sun steen skeea [στή σκιά]
   sunbathe eeleeotherapeea [ἡλιοθεραπεία]
   sunburn kamenos apo ton eeleeo [καμμένος
   ἀπό τόν ἥλιο]

sunglasses ya-lee*a* eelee*oo* [γιαλιά ἤλίου]
sunstroke eel*ee*assee [ἡλίαση]
suntan oil l*a*thee eelee*oo* [λάδι ἡλίου]
Sunday Keereea*kee* [Κυριακή]
supermarket to supermarket [τό σούπερ μάρκετ]
supper to th*ee*pno [τό δεῖπνο]
sure: I'm not sure then *ee*me veveos [δέν εἶμαι βέβαιος]; **sure!** veveos! [βεβαίως!]
are you sure? *ee*sse veveos? [εἶσαι βέβαιος;]
surfboard to kano [τό κανό]
surfing: to go surfing p*a*o serfeeng [πάω σέρφινγκ]
surname ep*ee*th*e*to [ἐπίθετο]
swearword mee*a* vreesse*a* [μιά βρισιά]
sweat *(verb)* eethrono [ἱδρώνω]
sweet: it's too sweet *ee*ne pol*ee* gleeko [εἶναι πολύ γλυκό]
(dessert) ep*ee*thorpeeo [ἐπιδόρπιο]
sweets karam*e*les [καραμέλες]
swerve: I had to swerve ep*re*pe na parekl*ee*no [ἔπρεπε νά παρεκλίνω]
swim: I'm going for a swim p*a*o ya kol*ee*mbee [πάω γιά κολύμπι]
let's go for a swim p*a*me ya kol*ee*mbee [πάμε γιά κολύμπι]
swimming costume to ma-ye-*o* [τό μαγιό]
switch o thee*a*koptees [ὁ διακόπτης]
to switch on/off an*a*vo/sv*ee*no [ἀνάβω/σβήνω]
table to trap*e*zee [τό τραπέζι]
a table for 4 ena trap*e*zee ya t*e*sserees [ἕνα τραπέζι γιά τέσσερις]
table wine epeetrap*e*zeeo krass*ee* [ἐπιτραπέζιο κρασί]
take p*e*rno [παίρνω]
can I take this with me? bor*o* na p*a*ro afto maz*ee* moo? [μπορῶ νά πάρω αὐτό μαζί μου;]
will you take me to the airport? bor*ee*te na me p*a*rete sto a-erothrom*ee*o? [μπορεῖτε νά μέ πάρετε στό ἀεροδρόμειο;]

how long will it take? posseen ora tha paree?
[πόσην ώρα θά πάρει;]
somebody has taken my bags kapeeos peere
tees valeedzes moo [κάποιος πῆρε τῖς βαλίτσες
μου]
can I take you out tonight? boro na se paro
exo seemera to vrathee? [μπορῶ νά σέ πάρω ἔξω
σήμερα τό βράδι;]
talcum powder poothra talk [πούδρα τάλκ]
talk *(verb)* meelo [μιλῶ]
tall pseelos [ψηλός]
tampons tampon [ταμπόν]
tan mavreesma apo toneeleeo [μαύρισμα ἀπό τόν
ἥλιο]
I want to get a tan thelo na mavreesso [θέλω
νά μαυρίσω]
tank *(of car)* to depozeeto [τό ντεπόζιτο]
tap ee vreessee [ἡ βρίση]
tape ee teneea [ἡ ταινία]
tape-recorder to magneetofono [τό
μαγνητόφωνο]
tariff tareefa [ταρίφα]
taste *(noun)* ye-fssee [γεύση]
can I taste it? boro na to thokeemasso? [μπορῶ
νά τό δοκιμάσω;]
it tastes horrible/very nice ekhee apesseea
ye-fssee/polee orea [ἔχει ἀπαίσια γεύση/πολύ
ὡραῖα]
taxi ena taxee [ἕνα ταξί]
will you get me a taxi? tha moo kalessete ena
taxee? [θά μου καλέσετε ἕνα ταξί;]
where can I get a taxi? poo boro na vro ena
taxee? [πού μπορῶ νά βρῶ ἕνα ταξί;]
taxi-driver o taxeedzees [ὁ ταξιτζής]
tea tssaee [τσάϊ]
could I have a cup/pot of tea? boro na ekho
ena fleedzanee/meea tsaye-era tssaee? [μπορῶ
νά ἔχω ἕνα φλιτζάνι/μιά τσαγιέρα τσάϊ;]
with milk/lemon me gala/lemone [μέ
γάλα/λεμόνι]

teach: could you teach me? borees na me
theethaxees? [μπορείς νά μέ διδάξεις;]
   could you teach me Greek? borees na me
theethaxees eleeneeka? [μπορείς νά μέ διδάξεις
Ἑλληνικά;]

teacher o thaskalos [ὁ δάσκαλος]

telegram ena teelegrafeema [ἕνα τηλεγράφημα]
   I want to send a telegram thelo na steelo ena
teelegrafeema [θέλω νά στήλω ἕνα
τηλεγράφημα]

telephone *(noun)* to teelefono [τό τηλέφωνο]
   can I make a phone-call? boro na
teelefoneesso? [μπορῶ νά τηλεφωνήσω;]
   can I speak to Maria? boro na meeleesso stee
Maria [μπορῶ νά μιλήσω στῆ Μαρία]
   could you get the number for me? boreete
na moo parete ton areethmo? [μπορεῖτε νά μου
πάρετε τόν ἀριθμό;]
   telephone directory o teelefoneekos
katalogos [ὁ τηλεφωνικός κατάλογος]

» *TRAVEL TIP: two types of phone; one with the same
dialling method as in the UK; but if you don't get
a tone when you lift the receiver then put money
in before dialling; code for UK is 0044, dropping
first 0 of UK area code*

television ee teeleorassee [ἡ τηλεόραση]
   I'd like to watch television thathela na tho
teeleorassee [θάθελα νά δῶ τηλεόραση]

tell: could you tell me where . . .? boreete na
moo peete poo . . .? [μπορεῖτε νά μου πῆτε
ποῦ . . .;]

temperature *(weather etc)* ee thermokrasseea
[ἡ θερμοκρασία]
   he's got a temperature ekhee peereto [ἔχει
πυρετό]

temple o naos [ὁ ναός]

tennis tennis [τέννις]
   tennis court ye-petho tennis [γήπεδο τέννις]
   tennis racket raketa tennis [ρακέτα τέννις]
   tennis ball bala too tennis [μπάλλα τοῦ τέννις]

tent ee ten̄ta [ή τέντα]
terminus to terma [τό τέρμα]
terrible fovero [φοβερό]
terrific exereteeko [ἐξεραιτικό]
than apo [ἀπό]
  bigger/older than ... megaleeteros/
  megaleeteros apo ...
  [μεγαλύτερος/μεγαλύτερος ἀπό ...]
thanks, thank you efkhareesto [εὐχαριστῶ]
  no thank you okhee efkhareesto [ὄχι ...]
  thank you very much efkhareesto polee
  [εὐχαριστῶ πολύ]
  thank you for your help efkhareesto ya teen
  voeetheea sas [εὐχαριστῶ γιά τήν βοήθειά σας]
  YOU MAY THEN HEAR ...
  parakalo *you're welcome*
that ekeeno [ἐκεῖνο]
  that man/that table ekeenos o
  anthras/ekeeno to trapezee [ἐκεῖνος ὁ
  ἄνδρας/ἐκεῖνο τό τραπέζι]
  I would like that one thathela ekeeno
  [θἄθελα ἐκεῖνο]
  how do you say that? pos to lene ekeeno? [πῶς
  τό λέτε ἐκεῖνο;]
  I think that ... nomeezo otee [νομίζω ὅτι ...]
the o, ee, to [ὁ, ή, τό]; *(plural)* ee, ee, ta
  [οί, οί, τά]
theatre to theatro [τό θέατρο]
their toos [τούς]
  it's their bag/it's theirs eene ee tssanda
  toos/eene theekeea toos [εἶναι ή τσάντα
  τους/εἶναι δικιά τους]
them: I've lost them toos, tees, ta ekhassa
  [τους, τίς, τά ἔχασα]
  with them mazee toos [μαζί τους]
  who? – them pee-ee? aftee, aftes, afta [ποιοί;
  αὐτοί, αὐτές, αὐτά]
then tote [τότε]
there ekee [ἐκεῖ]; **how do I get there?** postha
  pao ekee? [πῶς θά πάω ἐκεῖ;]

is there . . ./are there . . .? eeparkhee . . ./
eeparkhoon . . .? [ὑπάρχει . . ./ὑπάρχουν . . .;]
there is . . ./there are . . . eeparkhee . . ./
eeparkhoon . . . [ὑπάρχει . . ./ὑπάρχουν . . .]
there you are *(giving something)* oreeste
[ὁρίστε]
these aft*ee*, aft*es*, aft*a* [αὐτοί, αὐτές, αὐτά]
  these apples aft*a* ta m*ee*la [αὐτά τά μήλα]
  can I take these? boro na p*a*ro aft*a* [μπορῶ νά
  πάρω αὐτά]
  these people aft*ee* ee *a*nthropee [αὐτοί οἱ
  ἄνθρωποι]
  these bags aft*es* ee ts*a*ndes [αὐτές οἱ τσάντες]
they aft*ee*, aft*es*, aft*a* [αὐτοί, αὐτές, αὐτά]
  they are . . . eene . . . [εἶναι . . .]
thick pakh*ee* [παχύ]
  (stupid) khaz*os* [χαζός]
thief o kleft*ees* [ὁ κλέφτης]
thigh o m*ee*ros [ὁ μηρός]
thin athee*na*tos [ἀδύνατος]
thing pr*a*gma [πρᾶγμα]
  I've lost all my things *e*khassa *o*la moo ta
  pr*a*gmata [ἔχασα ὅλα μου τά πράγματα]
think sk*e*ptome [σκέπτομαι]
  I'll think it over *tha* to skef-th*o* [θά τό σκεφθῶ]
  I think so/I don't think so nom*ee*zo/then
  nom*ee*zo [νομίζω/δέν νομίζω]
third *(adjective)* tr*ee*tos [τρίτος]
thirsty theepss*a*zmenos [διψασμένος]
  I'm thirsty theeps*o* [διψῶ]
this aft*os*, aft*ee*, aft*o* [αὐτός, αὐτή, αὐτό]
  this hotel/this street aft*o* to
  ksenothokh*ee*o/aft*os* o thr*o*mos [αὐτό τό
  ξενοδοχεῖο/αὐτός ὁ δρόμος]
  can I have this one? boro na *e*kho aft*o* eth*o*?
  [μπορῶ νά ἔχω αὐτό ἐδῶ;]
  this is my wife/this is Mr . . . aft*ee* eene ee
  ye-n*e*ka moo/aft*os* eene o k*ee*reeos . . . [αὐτή
  εἶναι ἡ γυναίκα μου/αὐτός εἶναι ὁ Κύριος . . .]
  is this . . .? eene aft*o* . . .? [εἶναι αὐτό . . .;]

those *see* **these**

  no, not these, those! okhee, okhee aft*a*, ek*ee*na! [ὄχι, ὄχι αὐτά, ἐκεῖνα!]

thread *(noun)* mee*a* klosst*ee* [μιά κλωστή]

throat o lem*os* [ὁ λεμός]

throttle *(motorbike, boat)* gazee [γκάζι]

through the*a* m*e*ssoo [διά μέσου]

throw *(verb)* reekhno [ρίχνω]

thumb o and*ee*kheeras [ὁ ἀντίχειρας]

thunder *(noun)* ee vrond*ee* [ἡ βροντή]

  thunderstorm kakokere*ea* [κακοκαιρία]

Thursday Pemtee [Πέμπτη]

ticket to eesseet*ee*reeo [τό εἰσιτήριο]

  (cloakroom) o areeth*m*os [ὁ ἀριθμός]

tie *(necktie)* ee gravata [ἡ γραβάτα]

tight *(clothes)* steno [στενό]

tights kaltss*on* [καλτσόν]

time ora, khron*os* [ὥρα, χρόνος]

  what's the time? tee ora eene? [τί ὥρα εἶναι;]

  I haven't got time then *e*kho khrono [δέν ἔχω χρόνο]

  for the time being ya teen ora [γιά τήν ὥρα]

  this time/last time/next time aft*ee* tee fora/teen perasm*e*nee fora/teen *a*lee fora [αὐτή τή φορά/τήν περασμένη φορά/τήν ἄλλη φορά]

  3 times trees for*es* [τρεῖς φορές]

  have a good time kal*ee* theeaskethassee [καλή διασκέδαση]

  timetable to programa [τό πρόγραμμα]

» *TRAVEL TIP: how to tell the time*

  it's one o'clock *ee*ne ee ora m*ee*a [εἶναι ἡ ὥρα μία]

  it's two/three/four/five/six o'clock *ee*ne ee ora the*e*o/trees/t*e*sserees/pende/exee [εἶναι ἡ ὥρα δύο/τρεῖς/τέσσερις/πέντε/ἕξι]

  it's 5/10/20/25 past seven eene ept*a* ke pende/the*k*a/*ee*kossee/*ee*kosse pende [εἶναι ἑπτά καί πέντε/δέκα/εἴκοσι/εἴκοσι πέντε]

  it's quarter past eight/eight fifteen *ee*ne okto ke t*e*tarto/okto ke th*e*ka pende [εἶναι ὀκτώ

καί τέταρτο/όκτώ καί δέκα πέντε]
it's half past nine/nine thirty eene enea ke
meessee/enea ke treeanda [εἶναι ἐννέα καί
μισή/ἐννέα καί τριάντα]
it's 25/20/10/5 to ten eene theka para eekosse
pende/eekossee/theka/pende [εἶναι δέκα παρά
εἴκοσι πέντε/εἴκοσι/δεκα/πέντε]
it's quarter to eleven/10.45 eeneendeka para
tetarto/endeka ke saranda pende [εἶναι ἔντεκα
παρά τέταρτο/ἔντεκα καί σαράντα πέντε]
it's twelve o'clock eene eeora thotheka [εἶναι
ἡ ὥρα δώδεκα]
tin *(can)* meea konsserva [μιά κονσέρβα]
tin-opener to aneekteeree [τό ἀνοιχτήρι]
tip *(noun)* to feelethoreema [τό φιλοδώρημα]
is the tip included? pereelamvanete to
feelothoreema? [περιλαμβάνεται τό
φιλοδώρημα;]
» *TRAVEL TIP: tip the same people as in UK*
tired koorasmenos [κουρασμένος]
I'm tired eeme koorasmenos [εἶμαι
κουρασμένος]
tissues khartomantheela [χαρτομάνδηλα]
to: to Crete/England ye-a teen
Kreetee/Angleea [γιά τή Κρήτη/'Αγγλία]
toast tost [τόστ]
tobacco kapnos [καπνός]
tobacconist's to kapnopoleeo [τό καπνοπωλεῖο]
» *TRAVEL TIP: buy tobacco from street kiosks called*
'to pereeptero' [τό περίπτερο]; *see* **kiosk**
today seemera [σήμερα]
toe to thakteelo too potheeoo [τό δάκτυλο τοῦ
ποδιοῦ]
together mazee [μαζί]
we're together eemaste mazee [εἴμαστε μαζί]
can we pay all together? boroome na
pleerosome ola mazee? [μπορούμε νά
πληρώσωμε ὅλα μαζί;]
toilet ee tooaleta [ἡ τουαλέττα]
where are the toilets? poo ene ee tooaleta?

[πού εἶναι ἡ τουαλέττα;]
I have to go to the toilet prepee na pao stee
tooaleta [πρέπει νά πάω στή τουαλέττα]
there's no toilet paper then eeparkhee
khartee tooaletas [δέν ὑπάρχει χαρτί
τουαλέτας]
» *TRAVEL TIP: see* **public**
tomato domata [ἡ τομάτα]
   tomato ketchup ketchup [κέτσαπ]
   tomato juice domatozoomo [τοματόζουμο]
tomorrow avreeo [αὔριο]
   tomorrow morning/tomorrow afternoon/
   tomorrow evening avreeo to proee/avreeo to
   apoye-vma/avreeo to vrathee [αὔριο τό πρωΐ/
   αὔριο τό ἀπόγευμα/αὔριο τό βράδι]
   the day after tomorrow methavreeo
   [μεθαύριο]
   see you tomorrow tha se thoavreeo [θά σέ δῶ
   αὔριο]
ton enas tonos [ἕνας τόνος]
» *TRAVEL TIP: 1 ton = 1016 kilos*
tongue ee glossa [ἡ γλῶσσα]
tonic (water) tonic [τόνικ]
tonight seemera to vrathee [σήμερα τό βράδυ]
tonne enas tonnos [ἕνας τόννος]
» *TRAVEL TIP: 1 tonne = 1000 kilos = metric ton*
tonsilitis ameegthaleetees [ἀμυγδαλίτις]
too polee [πολύ]; *(also)* epeessees [ἐπίσης]
   that's too much afto eene para polee [αὐτό
   εἶναι πάρα πολύ]
tool ergaleeo [ἐργαλεῖο]
tooth to thondee [τό δόντι]
   I've got toothache ekho ponothondo [ἔχω
   πονόδοντο]
   toothbrush ee othondovoortssa
   [ἡ ὀδοντόβουρτσα]
   toothpaste ee othondokrema [ἡ ὀδοντόκρεμα]
top: on top of . . . pano apo . . . [πάνω ἀπό . . .]
   on the top floor sto pano patoma [στό πάνω
   πάτωμα]

at the top stee korfee [στή κορφή]
total *(noun)* to seenolo [τό σύνολο]
tough *(meat)* skleero [σκληρό]
tour *(noun)* ee pereeotheea [ή περιοδία]
  we'd like to go on a tour of the island
  *the*lome na pame pereeotheea sto neessee
  [θέλομε νά πᾶμε περιοδία στό νησί]
  we're touring around pereeothevome
  [περιοδεύομε]
tourist o tooreestas [ό τουρίστας]
  I'm a tourist eeme tooreestas [εἶμαι τουρίστας]
  tourist office grafeeo tooreesmoo [γραφεῖο
  τουρισμοῦ]
tow *(verb)* reemoolko [ρυμουλκῶ]
  can you give me a tow? borees na me
  reemoolkeessees? [μπορεῖς νά μέ ρυμουλκήσεις;]
  towrope skheenee reemoolkeesseos [σχοινί
  ρυμουλκήσεως]
towards pros [πρός]
  he was coming straight towards me
  erkhondan kat' eftheean pros ta pano moo
  [ἐρχόνταν κατ' εὐθεῖαν πρός τά πάνω μου]
towel ee petsseta [ή πετσέτα]
town ee polee [ή πόλη]
  in town stee polee [στή πόλη]
  would you take me into the town? boreete
  na me parete stee polee? [μπορεῖτε νά μέ πάρετε
  στή πόλη;]
traditional patroparathotos [πατροπαράδοτος]
  a traditional Greek meal ena patroparathoto
  Eleeneeko fageeto [ἕνα πατροπαράδοτο
  Ἑλληνικό φαγητό]
traffic ee keekloforeea [ή κυκλοφορία]
  traffic lights fanareea trokheas [φανάρια
  τροχαίας]
train to treno [τό τραῖνο]
tranquillizers katapraeendeeka
  [καταπραϋντικά]
translate metefrazo [μεταφράζω]
  would you translate that for me? boreete na

moo metafrassete afto? [μπορείτε νά μου
μεταφράσετε αὐτό;]
transmission *(of car)* ee takh**ee**teetes [οἱ
ταχύτητες]
travel agent's praktoreeo taxeeth**ee**on
[πρακτορεῖο ταξιδίων]
traveller's cheque taxeetheeoteek**ee** epeetag**ee**
[ταξιδιωτική ἐπιταγή]
tree to th**e**nthro [τό δένδρο]
tremendous th**a**vmasseea [θαυμάσια]
trim: just a trim, please fresska**r**eesma mono,
parakal**o** [φρεσκάρισμα μόνο, παρακαλῶ]
trip *(noun)* to tax**ee**thee [τό ταξίδι]
we want to go on a trip to Hydra th**e**lome na
pame ena taxeethee steen Eethra [θέλομε νά
πάμε ἕνα ταξίδι στήν Ὕδρα]
trouble *(noun)* enokhleessee [ἐνόχληση]
**I'm having trouble with . . . (the
steering/my back)** ekho provleemata
me . . . (to teemonee/teen platee moo) [ἔχω
προβλήματα μέ . . . (τό τιμόνι/τήν πλάτη μου)]
trousers to pantalonee [τό πανταλόνι]
true al**ee**theeno [ἀληθινό]
it's not true then **ee**ne al**ee**theea [δέν εἶναι
ἀλήθεια]
trunks *(swimming)* to mayee-o [τό μαγιό]
try *(verb)* thok**ee**mazo [δοκιμάζω]
please try parakal**o** thokeem**a**ste [παρακαλῶ
δοκιμάστε]
can I try it on? boro na to thokeem**a**sso p**a**no
moo? [μπορῶ νά τό δοκιμάσω πάνω μου;]
T-shirt to blooza**ee** [τό μπλουζάκι]
Tuesday Tr**ee**tee [Τρίτη]
turn: where do we turn off? poo th**a**
str**ee**psome? [πού θά στρίψομε;]
he turned without indicating estreepse
khor**ee**s na val**ee** s**ee**ma [ἔστριψε χωρίς νά βάλει
σῆμα]
twice th**ee**o fores [δυό φορές]
twice as much ta theepl**a** [τά διπλά]

twin beds the*eo* krevat*eea* [δύο κρεβάτια]
typewriter ee grafomeekhan*ee* [ή γραφομηχανή]
typical teepeek*o* [τυπικό]
tyre la*ss*teekho [λάστιχο]
I need a new tyre khree*a*zome ken*oo*ryee-o
la*ss*teekho [χρήάζομε καινούργιο λάστιχο]
» *TRAVEL TIP: tyre pressures*

lb/sq in	18	20	22	24	26	28	30
kg/sq cm	13	1.4	15	1.7	1.8	2	2.1

ugly *a*skheemos [ἄσχημος]
ulcer *e*lkos [ἕλκος]
Ulster Vore*eos* Irlanth*ee*a [Βόρειος, 'Ιρλανδία]
umbrella me*ea* ombr*e*la [μιά όμπρέλλα]
uncle: my uncle o *thee*os moo [ό θεῖος μου]
uncomfortable *a*volos [ἄβολος]
unconscious an*ess*th*ee*tos [ἀναίσθητος]
under ap*o* kat*o* [ἀπό κάτω]
underdone meessopseem*e*no [μισοψημένο]
underground *(rail)* o eepogeeos [ό ὑπόγειος]
understand: I understand katalaveno
[καταλαβαίνω]
I don't understand then katalaveno [δέν
καταλαβαίνω]
do you understand? katalavenees?
[καταλαβαίνεις;]
undo le*e*no [λύνω]
unfriendly mee feeleek*o*s [μή φιλικός]
unhappy theesteekheesm*e*nos [δυστυχισμένος]
United States Inomenes Poleetee-es
['Ηνωμένες Πολιτεῖες]
unlock ksekleethono [ξεκλειδώνω]
until m*e*khree [μέχρι]
until next year m*e*khree too khron*oo* [μέχρι
τοῦ χρόνου]
unusual asseen*eeth*eestos [ἀσυνήθιστος]
up p*a*no [πάνω]
he's not up yet then ks*ee*pneesse ak*o*mee [δέν
ξύπνησε ἀκόμη]
what's up? tee g*ee*netee? [τί γίνεται;]
upside-down ta p*a*no kat*o* [τά πάνω κάτω]

upstairs pano [πάνω]
urgent epeegon [ἐπείγων]
us mas [μας]
use: can I use . . .? boro na khreessemopee-
   eesso . . .? [μπορῶ νά χρησιμοποιήσω . . .;]
useful khreesseemos [χρήσιμος]
usual seeneetheesmeno [συνηθισμένο]
   as usual opos seeneethos [ὅπως συνήθως]
usually seeneethos [συνήθως]
U-turn strofee epee topoo [στροφή ἐπί τόπου]
vacancy kenee thessee [κενή θέση]
   do you have any vacancies? ekhete kenes
   thessees? [ἔχετε κενές θέσεις;]
vacate (room) atheeazo [ἀδειάζω]
vaccination envoleeasmos [ἐμβολιασμός]
vacuum flask to thermos [τό θέρμος]
valid engeeros [ἔγκυρος]
   how long is it valid for? ya posso eeskhee-ee?
   [γιά πόσο ἰσχύει;]
valuable poleeteemos [πολύτιμος]
   will you look after my valuables? tha
   proseksete ta teemalfee moo? [θά προσέξετε τά
   τιμαλφῆ μου;]
value ee axeea [ἡ ἀξία]
valve ee valveetha [ἡ βαλβίδα]
van to trokhospeeto [τό τροχόσπιτο]
   (delivery) to forteego [τό φορτηγό]
vanilla vaneeleea [βανίλια]
varicose veins fleveetees [φλεβίτης]
veal veethelo [βιδέλο]
vegetables lakhaneeka [λαχανικά]
vegetarian khortofagos [χορτοφάγος]
ventilator o anemeesteeras [ὁ ἀνεμιστήρας]
very polee [πολύ]
   very much para polee [πάρα πολύ]
via theea messoo [διά μέσου]
village to khoreeo [τό χωριό]
vine ee kleematareea [ἡ κληματαριά]
vinegar to kseethee [τό ξύδι]
vineyard to ambelee [τό ἀμπέλι]

vintage o treegos [ὁ τρύγος]
violent vee-eos [βίαιος]
visibility oratotees [ὁρατότης]
visit *(verb)* epeeskeptome [ἐπισκέπτομαι]
vodka votka [βότκα]
voice fonee [φωνή]
voltage volt [βόλτ]
waist messee [μέση]

» *TRAVEL TIP: waist measurements*

UK	24	26	28	30	32	34	36	38
Greece	61	66	71	76	80	87	91	97

wait: will we have to wait long? *th*a prepee na
pereemenoome polee? [θά πρέπει νά
περιμένουμε πολύ;]
 wait for me pereemene me [περίμενέ με]
 I'm waiting for a friend/my wife pereem*e*no
 ena *fee*lo/tee yeeneka moo [περιμένω ἕνα
 φίλο/τή γυναίκα μου]
waiter o serveetoros [ὁ σερβιτόρος]
 waiter! garson! [γκαρσόν!]

» *TRAVEL TIP: it is no longer acceptable (as some
books say) to clap your hands for the waiter*

waitress serveetora [σερβιτόρα]
 waitress! thespeen*ee*s! [δεσποινίς]
wake: will you wake me up at 7.30? bor*ee*te na
me kseepn*ee*ssete stees epta ke meess*ee*?
[μπορεῖτε νά μέ ξυπνήσετε στίς 7 καί μισή;]
Wales Ooaleea [Οὐαλλία]
walk: can we walk there? bor*oo*me na p*a*me
perpatontas ek*ee*? [μπορούμε νά πᾶμε
περπατώντας ἐκεῖ;]
 are there any good walks around here?
 eeparkhoon ore-es voltes etho yee-ro?
 [ὑπάρχουν ὡραῖες βόλτες ἐδῶ γύρω;]
 walking shoes papootsseea pereep*a*too
 [παπούτσια περιπάτου]
 walking stick to bast*oo*nee [τό μπαστούνι]
wall o t*ee*khos [ὁ τοῖχος]
wallet to portof*o*lee [τό πορτοφόλι]
want: I want a … *the*lo ena … [θέλω ἕνα …]

I want to talk to the consul thelo na
meeleesso ston proxeno [θέλω νά μιλήσω στόν
πρόξενο]
  what do you want? tee thelees? [τί θέλεις;]
I don't want to then thelo na [δέν θέλω νά]
he wants to . . . thelee na . . . [θέλει νά . . .]
warm khleearos [χλιαρός]
warning proeethopee-eessee [προειδοποίηση]
was: I was/he was/it was eemoon/eessoon/
eetan [ἤμουν/ἤσουν/ἦταν]
wash: can you wash these for me? boreete na
moo pleenete afta? [μπορεῖτε νά μοῦ πλύνετε
αὐτά;]
  where can I wash? poo boro na pleetho? [ποῦ
μπορῶ νά πλυθῶ;]
  washing powder aporeepandeeko
[ἀπορυπαντικό]
washer (for nut) ee rothela [ἡ ροδέλλα]
wasp ee sfeeka [ἡ σφῆκα]
watch (wrist-) to roloee [τό ρολόϊ]
  will you watch my bags for me? tha
boroossate na moo prosekhete tees tsandes? [θά
μπορούσατε νά μοῦ προσέξετε τίς τσάντες;]
  watch out! prossekhe![πρόσεχε!]
water to nero [τό νερό]
  can I have some water? boro nakho leego
nero? [μπορῶ νἄχω λίγο νερό;]
  hot and cold running water zesto ke kreeo
trekhoomeno nero [ζεστό καί κρύο τρεχούμενο
νερό]
  waterproof atheeavrokho [ἀδιάβροχο]
  waterskiing thalasseeo skee [θαλάσσιο σκύ]
way: we'd like to eat the Greek way thelo na
fao Eleeneeko fayeto [θέλω νά φάω Έλληνικό
φαγητό]
  could you tell me the way to . . .? boreete na
moo peete to thromo ya . . .? [μπορεῖτε νά μου
πῆτε τό δρόμο γιά . . .;]
  for answers see **where**
we emees [ἐμεῖς]; **we are** eemaste [εἴμαστε]

weak ath*ee*natos [ἀδύνατος]
weather o keros [ο καιρός]
  what filthy weather! tee ap*ee*sseeos keros
  [τί ἀπαίσιος καιρός]
  what's the weather forecast? tee l*e*-ee to
  meteoroloyeeko thelt*ee*o? [τί λέει τό
  μετεωρολογικό δελτεῖο;]
  YOU MAY THEN HEAR . . .
  *th*a kanee *z*estee *it's going to be hot*
  *th*a vr*ee*ksee *it's going to rain*
Wednesday Tetartee [Τετάρτη]
week mee*a* evthom*a*tha [μιά ἑβδομάδα]
  a week today/tomorrow se mee*a*
  evthom*a*tha apo s*ee*mera/*a*vreeo [σέ μιά
  ἑβδομάδα ἀπό σήμερα/αὔριο]
  at the weekend to Savatok*ee*reeako [τό
  Σαββατοκύριακο]
weight to b*a*ros [τό βάρος]
well: I'm not feeling well th*e*n est*ha*nome kala
  [δέν αἰσθάνομαι καλά]
  he's not well th*e*n *ee*ne kala [δέν εἶναι καλά]
  how are you? very well, thanks tee k*a*nees?
  pol*ee* kala efkhareesto [τί κάνεις; πολύ καλά
  εὐχαριστῶ]
  you speak English very well meel*a*te
  Angleeka pol*ee* kala [μιλάτε 'Αγγλικά πολύ
  καλά]
wellingtons ee galotses [οἱ γαλότσες]
Welsh Ooalos [Οὐαλλός]
were: you were *ee*ssoon [ἤσουν]
  we were *ee*maste [ἤμαστε]
  you were *(plural, polite form)* *ee*ssaste
  [ἤσαστε] **they were** *ee*tan [ἤταν]
west theet*ee*ka [δυτικά]
West Indies Theet*ee*kes Inth*ee*-es [Δυτικές
  'Ινδίες]
wet eegros [ὑγρός]
  wet suit mee*a* forma katath*ee*seeos [μία φόρμα
  καταδύσεως]
what tee [τί]

what is that? tee*eene* ekee*no?* [τί εἶναι ἐκεῖνο;]

what for? ya pee*o* logo? [γιά ποιό λόγο;]

wheel ee rotha [ἡ ρόδα]

when pote [πότε]

    when is breakfast? pote *eene* to proyevma?
[πότε εἶναι τό πρόγευμα;]

    when we arrived *o*tan *fthassame* [ὅταν
φθάσαμε]

where poo [ποῦ]

    where is the post office? poo *eene* to
takheethrom*eeo?* [ποῦ εἶναι τό ταχυδρομεῖο;]

    YOU MAY THEN HEAR...

    *ee*seea *straight on*

    o th*efteros* thromos areestera *the second left*

    o protos thromos thexe*ea first right*

    se the*eo* kheelee*ometra two kilometres further*

which pee*os* [ποιός]

    which one? pee*o* ap' ola? [ποιό ἀπ' ὅλα;]

    YOU MAY THEN HEAR...

    aft*o this one* ekee*no that one*

whisky whisky [οὔϊσκι]

white *a*spro [ἄσπρο]

who pee*os* [ποιός]

    YOU MAY THEN HEAR...

    aft*os him* aft*ee her*

whose peean*oo* [ποιανοῦ]

    whose is this? peean*oo eene* aft*o?* [ποιανοῦ
εἶναι αὐτό;]

    YOU MAY THEN HEAR...

    eene too Yan*ee it's John's*

    eene theek*o* moo *it's mine*

why? yat*ee?* [γιατί;]

    why not? yat*ee* okhee? [γιατί ὄχι;]

wide plat*ee* [πλατύ]

wife: my wife ee seezeeg*os* moo [ἡ σύζυγός μου]

will: when will it be finished? pote *tha*
telee*ossee?* [πότε θά τελειώσει;]

    will you do it? bor*eete* na to k*a*nete? [μπορεῖτε
νά τό κάνετε;]; **I will come back** *tha*
epeestr*e*pso [θά ἐπιστρέψω]

wind o *a*nem*os* [ὁ ἄνεμος]
window to pa*ra*th*ee*ro [τό παράθυρο]
   near the window kon*ta* sto pa*ra*th*ee*ro [κοντά στό παράθυρο]
windscreen to bar-pr*ee*z [τό μπάρ-πρίζ]
   windscreen wipers *ee* *ee*alo*ka*th*a*r*ee*st*ee*r*es* [οἱ ὑαλοκαθαριστῆρες]
windy f*ee*ss*a*ee pol*ee* [φυσάει πολύ]
wine to kr*a*ss*ee* [τό κρασί]
   can I see the wine list? bor*o* na tho ton kat*a*logo ton kras*ee*on? [μπορῶ νά δῶ τόν κατάλογο τῶν κρασιῶν;]
» *TRAVEL TIP: some well-known types of Greek wine are:*
   *a*spro krass*ee* [ἄσπρο κρασί] *white, dry or sweet*
   kokkino krass*ee* [κόκκινο κρασί] *red, dry or sweet*
   rets*ee*na [ρετσίνα] *resinated white wine, very strong and distinctive taste*
   ma*v*rothafn*ee* [μαυροδάφνη] *red dessert wine, very sweet*
   kok*ee*n*e*l*ee* [κοκκινέλι] *red wine sold on draught in* ½ *litre tin measures*
   bro*o*sko [μπροῦσκο] *red, very dry*
winter o kh*ee*m*o*nas [ὁ χειμώνας]
wire *e*na kalothe*e*o [ἕνα καλώδιο]
wish: best wishes pol*e*s efkh*e*s [πολλές εὐχές]
with maz*ee* [μαζί]
without khor*ee*s [χωρίς]
witness mart*ee*ras [μάρτυρας]
   will you act as a witness for me? bor*ee*s na *ee*se mart*ee*ra*s* moo? [μπορεῖς νά εἶσαι μαρτυράς μου;]
woman *ee* y*ee*n*e*ka [ἡ γυναῖκα]
   women *ee* y*ee*n*e*k*es* [οἱ γυναῖκες]
wonderful th*a*vm*a*ss*ee*os [θαυμάσιος]
won't: it won't start then ksek*ee*n*a*ee [δέν ξεκινάει]
wood to ks*ee*lo [τό ξύλο]; *(trees)* th*a*sos [δάσος]
wool mal*ee* [μαλλί]

word ee leksee [ή λέξη]
  I don't know that word then ksero aftee tee leksee [δέν ξέρω αὐτή τή λέξη]
work ergazome [ἐργάζομαι]
  it's not working then ergazete [δέν ἐργάζεται]
  I work in London ergazome sto lontheeno [ἐργάζομαι στό Λονδῖνο]
worry stenokhoreea [στενοχώρια]
  I'm worried about him stenokhoree-eme yafton [στενοχωριέμαι γιαὐτόν]
  don't worry meen aneesseekhees [μήν ἀνησυχεῖς]
worry beads to komboloee [τό κομπολόϊ]
worse: it's worse eene kheerotera [εἶναι χειρότερα]
  he's getting worse kheeroterevee [χειροτερεύει]
worst kheeroteros [χειρότερος]
worth: it's not worth that much then akseezee tosso polee [δέν ἀξίζει τόσο πολύ]
  is it worthwhile going? akseezee ton kopo na pame? [ἀξίζει τόν κόπο νά πάμε;]
wrap: could you wrap it up? boreete na to teeleeksete? [μπορεῖτε νά τό τυλίξετε;]
wrench ena kleethe [ἕνα κλειδί]
wrist o karpos [ὁ καρπός]
write grafo [γράφω]
  could you write it down? boreete na moo to grapsete? [μπορεῖτε νά μοῦ τό γράψετε;]
  I'll write to you tha soo grapso [θά σοῦ γράψω]
  writing paper epeestolokharto [ἐπιστολόχαρτο]
wrong lathos [λάθος]
  I think the bill's wrong nomeezo otee o logareeazmos eene lathos [νομίζω ὅτι ὁ λογαριασμός εἶναι λάθος]
  there's something wrong with ... egeene kapeeo lathos me ... [ἔγινε κάποιο λάθος μέ . . .]
  you're wrong kanees lathos [κάνεις λάθος]

sorry, wrong number seegnomee lathos areethmos [συγγνώμη, λάθος ἀριθμός]

X-ray ee akteenografeea [ἡ ἀκτινογραφία]

yacht to yot [τό γιώτ]

yard ee avlee [ἡ αὐλή]

» *TRAVEL TIP: 1 yard = 91.44 cms = 0.91 m*

year o khronos [ὁ χρόνος]
  this year/next year fetos/too khronoo [φέτος/τοῦ χρόνου]

yellow keetreeno [κίτρινο]

yes ne [ναί]

yesterday khthes [χθές]
  the day before yesterday prokhthes [προχθές]
  yesterday morning/afternoon khthes to proee/to apoyevma [χθές τό πρωΐ/τό ἀπόγευμα]

yet: is it ready yet? eeneeteemo? [εἶναι ἕτοιμο;]
  not yet okhee akomee [ὄχι ἀκόμη]

yoghurt to yaoortee [τό γιαούρτι]

you essee [ἐσύ]
  (plural, polite form) essees [ἐσεῖς]
  I like you maressees [μ' ἀρέσεις]
  with you mazee soo [μαζί σου]

» *TRAVEL TIP: the polite form is used in more formal situations*

young neos [νέος]

your theeko [δικό σου]
  (plural, polite form) theeko sas [δικό σας]
  is this your camera?, is this yours? aftee ee fotografeekee meekhanee eene theekee soo, eene theeko soo? [αὐτή ἡ φωτογραφική μηχανή εἶναι δική σου, εἶναι δικό σου;]

youth hostel ksenonas neon [ξενώνας νέων]

Yugoslavia Yungoslaveea [Γιουγκοσλαβία]

Yugoslavian Yungoslavos [Γιουγκοσλάβος]

zero meethen [μηδέν]
  below zero eepo to meethen [ὑπό τό μηδέν]

zip fermooar [φερμουάρ]

GREEK SIGNS AND NOTICES

ΑΙΘΟΥΣΑ ΑΝΑΜΟΝΗΣ *waiting room*

ΑΝΑΧΩΡΗΣΕΙΣ *departures*

ΑΝΟΙΚΤΟΝ *open*

ΑΠΑΓΟΡΕΥΕΤΑΙ Η ΕΙΣΟΔΟΣ *no entry*

ΑΠΑΓΟΡΕΥΕΤΑΙ Η ΚΟΛΥΜΒΗΣΗ *no swimming*

ΑΠΑΓΟΡΕΥΟΝΤΑΙ ΟΙ ΚΑΤΑΔΥΣΕΙΣ *no diving*

ΑΠΑΓΟΡΕΥΕΤΑΙ ΤΟ ΚΑΠΝΙΣΜΑ *no smoking*

ΑΠΑΓΟΡΕΥΕΤΑΙ Η ΛΗΨΗ ΦΩΤΟΓΡΑΦΙΩΝ *no photographs*

ΑΣΤΥΝΟΜΙΑ *police*

ΑΦΙΞΕΙΣ *arrivals*

ΔΙΟΔΙΑ *toll*

ΕΘΝΙΚΗ ΟΔΟΣ *motorway*

ΕΙΣΟΔΟΣ *entrance*

ΕΛΕΥΘΕΡΟΝ *vacant*

ΕΝΟΙΚΙΑΖΟΝΤΑΙ ΔΩΜΑΤΙΑ *rooms to let*

ΕΞΟΔΟΣ *exit*

ΕΞΟΔΟΣ ΚΙΝΔΥΝΟΥ *emergency exit*

ΕΙΣΙΤΗΡΙΑ *tickets*

ΖΕΣΤΟ *hot*

ΚΑΤΕΙΛΗΜΜΕΝΟ *engaged*

ΚΙΝΔΥΝΟΣ *danger*

ΚΛΕΙΣΤΟΝ *closed*

ΚΡΥΟ *cold*

ΜΗ ΕΓΓΙΖΕΤΕ *don't touch*

ΝΟΣΟΚΟΜΕΙΟ *hospital*

ΠΛΗΡΟΦΟΡΙΕΣ *information*

ΠΟΣΙΜΟ ΝΕΡΟ *drinking water*

ΠΡΟΣΟΧΗ *caution*

ΠΡΟΣΟΧΗ ΝΑΡΚΕΣ *caution mines*

ΡΕΣΕΨΙΟΝ *reception*

ΣΥΡΑΤΕ *pull*

ΤΑΜΕΙΟ *cash desk*

ΤΕΛΩΝΕΙΟ *customs*

ΤΟΥΑΛΕΤΕΣ *toilets*

ΩΘΗΣΑΤΕ *push*

```
 0  meethen [μηδέν]
 1  ena [ἕνα]
 2  theeo [δύο]
 3  treea [τρία]
 4  tessera [τέσσερα]
 5  pende [πέντε]
 6  exee [ἕξι]
 7  epta [ἑπτά]
 8  okto [ὀκτώ]
 9  enea [ἐννέα]
10  theka [δέκα]
11  endeka [ἕντεκα]
12  thotheka [δώδεκα]
13  thekatreea [δεκατρία]
14  thekatessera [δεκατέσσερα]
15  thekapende [δεκαπέντε]
16  theaexee [δεκαέξι]
17  thekaepta [δεκαεπτά]
18  thekaokto [δεκαοκτώ]
19  thekaenea [δεκαεννέα]
20  eekossee [εἴκοσι]
21  eekossee ena [εἴκοσι ἕνα]
22  eekossee theeo [εἴκοσι δύο]
23  eekossee treea [εἴκοσι τρία]
24  eekossee tessera [εἴκοσι τέσσερα]
25  eekossee pende [εἴκοσι πέντε]
26  eekossee exee [εἴκοσι ἕξι]
27  eekossee epta [εἴκοσι ἑπτά]
28  eekossee okto [εἴκοσι ὀκτώ]
29  eekossee enea [εἴκοσι ἐννέα]
30  treeanda [τριάντα]
31  treeanda ena [τριάντα ἕνα]
40  saranda [σαράντα]
50  peneenda [πενήντα]
60  exeenda [ἑξήντα]
```

70 evthomeenda [ἑβδομήντα]
80 ogthonda [ὀγδόντα]
90 eneneenda [ἐνενήντα]
100 ekato [ἑκατό]
101 ekaton ena [ἑκατόν ἔνα]
165 ekaton exeenda pende
   [ἑκατόν ἑξήντα πέντε]
200 theeakossea [διακόσια]
300 treeakosseea [τριακόσια]
1,000 kheeleea [χίλια]
2,000 theeo kheeleeathes [δύο χιλιάδες]
3,000 trees kheeleeathes [τρεῖς χιλιάδες]
4,655 tesserees kheeleeathes exakosseea
    peneenda pende

NB: *in Greek the comma is a decimal point; for
thousands use a full-stop, eg 6.000*

Dates: *to say the date in Greek just use the
ordinary number, eg:*

on the second of ... stees theeo ...

Exceptions are:

on the 1st of ... stees meea
on the 3rd of ... stees trees
on the 4th of ... stees tesserees
on the 13th of ... stees thekatrees
on the 14th of ... stees thekatesserees
on the 21st of ... stees eekossee meea
on the 23rd of ... stees eekossee trees
on the 24th of ... stees eekossee tesserees
on the 31st of ... stees treeanda meea

THE GREEK ALPHABET

Α	α	ἄλφα	ALFA	a *as in* Anne
Β	β	βῆτα	VITA	v
Γ	γ	γάμμα	GAMA	y *as in* yes
Δ	δ	δέλτα	THELTA	th *as in* that
Ε	ε	ἔψιλον	EPSILON	e *as in* end
Ζ	ζ	ζῆτα	ZITA	z *as in* zero
Η	η	ἦτα	ITA	ee
Θ	θ	θῆτα	THITA	th *as in* theatre
Ι	ι	γιῶτα	YOTA	ee
Κ	κ	κάπα	KAPA	k
Λ	λ	λάμδα	LAMTHA	l
Μ	μ	μί	MI	m
Ν	ν	νί	NI	n
Ξ	ξ	ξί	KSI	x
Ο	ο	ὄμικρον	OMIKRON	o
Π	π	πί	PE	p
Ρ	ρ	ρό	RO	r
Σ	σ, ς*	σίγμα	SIGMA	s
Τ	τ	ταῦ	TAF	t
Υ	υ	ὕψιλον	IPSILON	ee
Φ	φ	φί	FI	f
Χ	χ	χί	KHI	ch *as in* Scottish loch
Ψ	ψ	ψί	PSI	ps
Ω	ω	ὠμέγα	OMEGA	o

*used only at the end of a word